LIFE

OF

HENRY DUNSTER,

FIRST PRESIDENT OF HARVARD COLLEGE.

BY

REV. JEREMIAH CHAPLIN, D.D.

BOSTON:
JAMES R. OSGOOD AND COMPANY,
(LATE TICKNOR & FIELDS, AND FIELDS, OSGOOD, & CO.)
1872.

Boston:
Stereotyped and Printed by Rand, Avery, & Co.

PREFACE.

THE name of Henry Dunster, the first President of Harvard College, passed under a cloud of neglect about the year 1652, but without any fault of his own. His contemporaries, who had extolled his accomplishments and virtues until the fatal hour when he "fell" into certain "briars" of dissent from the established creed, then suddenly dropped him from their calendar of worthies, and he has never been really invited to resume his place.

Different writers in our day, especially Quincy[1] and Palfrey,[2] have indeed eulogized his character and services in eloquent words, but no special effort has been made to gather the scattered materials of his life into a fitting memorial, that the world might know what he was, what part he acted in laying the foundations of our civil and religious institutions, and what he was willing to suffer, with singular patience and charity, for the sake of truth, as he understood it.

A due examination will show that his character is one

[1] History of Harvard College. [2] History of New England.

of the most beautiful, as his history is one of the most touching, to be found in the early annals of New England. A singularly honest mind, which no promises and no persecutions could turn from his convictions, forced him into antagonism with brethren whom he loved, and made him the target for sharp arrows, ecclesiastical and civil, which sorely wounded his pure and sensitive spirit. Firm as a rock in the defence of his principles, he could never be roused to a fight with his adversaries. He bore his testimony calmly and manfully, in the fear of God and the love of truth, and then yielded to the storm which drove him into retirement.

From that retirement of more than two centuries, it is well that he should come forth to teach us of this generation the great duty of loyalty to conscience, and how to harmonize conscience and charity. A life which, says Palfrey, is "of the purest and noblest," is not, alas, so very common, that the world can afford to lose the benefit of its bright example.

In pursuance of our purpose, we have reviewed the conduct of our Puritan ancestors of Massachusetts, in their treatment of what they deemed heresy and sectarism, — a duty not altogether agreeable, but yet unavoidable if regard is had to the facts of history and the lessons of experience.

A letter of Dr. Watts informs us, that when Neal was blamed for "the freedom he had taken to expose the persecuting principles and practices of the first planters," in his History of New England, "he replied, that the fidelity of an historian required him to do what he had done." Similar is our apology, if apology is needed. The author, as of Puritan descent, may be supposed to take as favorable a view as possible, of the Puritan fathers of Massachusetts. While ready to extol their grand virtues, he would deal charitably with their grave faults. Yet these men were so truly great and good, that, better than most men, they can bear the exposure which historic justice necessitates. Subject their characters to as rigid an examination as we may, they yet command our love and veneration.

Then, too, it should not be forgotten, that the Puritans of New England were not sinners above all the American Colonists, in religious intolerance. Virginia certainly has nothing to boast over Massachusetts. She began her inquisitorial work at an earlier period. The Dutch of New York pursued the same course, though with unequal steps.

It was the grand mistake — to use the mildest term — of the Reformers generally, which may as well be confessed — of Calvin and Zwingle and Knox and Cranmer, and a host of other noble champions of Protestantism, that they were persecutors. They were untrue to their own principle of the right of private judgment. And so the Puritans of the new world, in one sense, came honestly by their intolerance. If not in the line of apostolical succession, it was by ecclesiastical tradition. And they would have thanked no one for setting up an apology for their conduct towards sectarists and errorists on the low ground of expediency or political necessity. They persecuted from principle. They verily thought they were doing God service. Persecution of heretics was using "the holy tactics of the sword." "The most perfect harmony," says Trumbull, "subsisted between the legislature and clergy; like Moses and Aaron,[1] they walked together in the most endearing friendship." And, in their view, Moses and Aaron, as symbolical of state and church, never "kissed each other" to such good purpose, as when they united in "Mount Zion" to maintain the gospel against antichrist. A dreadful mistake; but an honest one.

[1] The Rev. John Norton, in 1646, preached a sermon in Boston, on "Moses and Aaron kissing each other in the Mount of God," in which he urged the churches [Aaron] to send Delegates to the Synod which had been summoned by the General Court [Moses]. In 1661, Rev. James Noyes, of Newbury, whom Cotton Mather highly praises, wrote, under the title of, "Moses and Aaron: or, The Rights of Church and State," as follows: "Civil and sacred power did consist well in the same subject, and surely they are most subject to violence when at greatest distance from one another. Moses and Aaron have cause to embrace each other, and Israel both of them together." "It is needful that Magistrates should have power to preserve the Church from desolation, by taking away foxes and wolves &c. Magistrates have a just power to use the sword in their hands against any persons for the good of the Church and the glory of Christ's kingdom. . . . It appears by Paul's appealing unto Cæsar, that magistrates have power in some religious controversies; why not in all?" In 1684, an English minister wrote to Increase Mather: "I rejoice to hear of so sweet a harmony between Moses and Aaron, and such a joint pursuit after reformation." Mass. Hist. Col. Mather Papers. This was four years after the meetinghouse of the First Baptist Church of Boston, of which the Rev. Rollin H. Neale D.D. is now the senior pastor, was shut up by order of the General Court — a fine specimen of the "sweet harmony."

Probably no case could more clearly exhibit the inherent injustice of the New England theocracy in its dealings with dissentients, than that of Mr. Dunster. Here was no crazy reformer, "conscientiously contentious," as has been affirmed, falsely, we think, of Roger Williams, in boisterous collision with established opinions and institutions. Mr. Dunster craved but the bare privilege of expressing his honest thoughts, with no purpose of assailing or abusing others. He was no iconoclast. He was just the opposite. Thoroughly manly and courageous, he was yet gentle and courteous. But no, said the managers of the theocracy, he does not think as we do, and *says* so — away with him.

One of our own writers, whom the world delights to honor for his rare felicities of thought and style, has undertaken the brave task — we profoundly respect his courage — of defending the Puritan way of dealing with sectaries. Mr. Lowell's main argument is as follows: — "that John of Leyden had taught them how unendurable by the nostrils of honest men is the corruption of the right of private judgment in the evil and selfish hearts of men when no thorough mental training has developed the understanding and given the judgment its needful means of comparison and correction. They knew that liberty in the hands of unreasoning and feeble-minded persons (and all the worse if they are honest) means nothing more than the supremacy of their particular form of imbecility, means nothing less therefore than downright chaos, a Bedlam chaos of monomaniacs and bores." *

* Among my Books, p. 235.

But most assuredly our Puritan fathers could not have proceeded upon this principle in dealing with Mr. Dunster for his exercise of the right of private judgment. If "unreasoning and feeble-minded persons" must be held in with bit and bridle, here was a sectary possessed of "thorough mental training." But the Puritans drew no such distinctions, except that they evidently deemed the heretic who was capable of "comparison and correction" to be the more dangerous.

What could there be in him of Cambridge—in his opinions or his conduct—most remotely suggestive of him of Leyden? Verily it requires a brilliant imagination to convert the mild, cultured, devout Mr. Dunster, known to everybody as a good neighbor, an orderly citizen, a gentleman and a Christian, into a lineal descendant of the monster of Holland, with his traditional hoofs and horns. After fourteen years of proof that he was strong-minded and sound-hearted, it was altogether too late to make him out, of a sudden, "unendurable by the nostrils of honest men."

The case is just here. The Puritans believed that to them was specially intrusted, here in this western world, the safe-keeping of the pure gospel, its doctrines, ordinances and institutions. It was a religious duty to defend it against all dissidents and opposers, whether these were "unreasoning and feeble-minded persons," or those in whom a "thorough mental training had developed the understanding." They were bound to defend it by both spiritual and temporal weapons. The state was a divine instrument for guarding the church — their church — and punishing sectaries and schismatics. It was not at all a question of strong-minded or feeble-minded, but simply of contrary-minded. The Puritans were remorselessly impartial. Their method of dealing with Mr. Dunster abundantly proves this. He questioned their infallibility, and was punished for it.

In all this the Puritans acted as if orthodoxy had, by them, been fully and finally settled. The possibilities of future illumination were exhausted.

Dunster was also a Puritan; but he was a consistent one, in demanding for himself and all others the right of private judgment. He "boldly" defended this right for the Quakers. In so doing he acted up to the advice to the departing Pilgrims, of another John of Leyden, John Robinson, pastor of the Pilgrim church and "father of independency:" — "If God reveal anything to you by any other instrument of his, be as ready to receive it as ever you were to receive any truth by my ministry; for I am verily persuaded the Lord has more truth yet to break forth out of his holy word."

The Puritans in and around Boston unfortunately knew the whole truth. There was no more light to "break forth." Humble Mr. Dunster, President of the College and a learned Orientalist, felt that there was something more to be known, and opened his eyes to the light. Then this Massachusetts Galileo, for daring to look above his creed, and to proclaim what he thought a new discovery, was speedily summoned before the Puritan tribunals.

"Moses and Aaron" were all agog to punish him for using his eyes. But, unlike the illustrious seer of Pisa, he did not, to save himself, deny his belief, or utter it only in a whisper.

But while we thus speak of our Puritan fathers, we most heartily apply to them what the late Mr. Grote said so finely with reference to Sir Thomas More: "The spirit of persecution is no peculiar attribute of the pedant, the bigot or the fanatic, but may coëxist with the fairest graces of the human character." In fact, we have only repeated the opinion entertained of these men by eminent Puritans of a succeeding generation. Benjamin Colman, for nearly fifty years pastor of the Brattle-street Church, Boston, said, in a Fast-day sermon delivered in 1716: "If there were of old among our fathers any laws enacted, or judgments given, or executions done according to those laws, which have carried too much the face of cruelty and persecution, we ought to be greatly humbled for such errors of our fathers, and confess them to have been sinful; and blessed be God for the more catholic spirit of charity which now distinguishes us. Or if any of our fathers have dealt proudly in censuring and judging others who differed from them in modes of worship, let us their posterity the rather be clothed with humility, meekness and charity, preserving truth and holiness with the laudable zeal of our predecessors." And two years later, Cotton Mather wrote as follows: "In this capital city of Boston there are ten assemblies of Christians of different persuasions, who live so lovingly and peaceably together, doing all the offices of good neighborhood for one another in such a manner as may give a sensible rebuke to all the bigots of uniformity, and show them how consistent a variety of rites in religion may be with the tranquillity of human society, and may demonstrate to the world, that persecution for conscientious dissents in religion is an abomination of desolation, a thing whereof all wise and just men will say, 'Cursed be its anger, for it is fierce, and its wrath, for it is cruel.'"[1]

Gladly do we acknowledge the vast debt of gratitude we owe to the stern Puritans, who, with the more catholic Pilgrims, founded our institutions; who established a Church without a bishop, and a State without a king; but surely very much is due to the men, who, while sharing the general views of the Puritans, did, either by a bold spirit of resistance, or a patient spirit of endurance, put themselves in opposition to certain errors which marred the beauty and weakened the power of the Puritan character, and thus gave to mankind an example of Protestantism more accordant with its true genius. Such men in their own day are likely to be misunderstood and even slandered, because their testimony breaks rudely in upon the established order of society; but surely posterity, which enjoys and glories in the results of their work, ought to do something better than to perpetuate the reproaches which were heaped upon them by a less enlightened or less tolerant age.

[1] See Neal's History of New England.

In the preparation of this work, the original sources of information have been diligently examined. The Public Library of Boston, especially the Prince Collection, the libraries of the Massachusetts Historical Society and the Historic-Genealogical Society, of Boston, the State Library, including the State Archives, the University Library at Cambridge, and the Middlesex County Records have been searched for material, and have been of invaluable service. The author would acknowledge the courtesy of the Historical Society and the Historic-Genealogical Society in granting the use of valuable manuscripts, never before published. And in this connection, he takes the liberty to make special mention of Dr. S. A. Green, Librarian of the former, and Jeremiah Colburn, Esq., one of the officers of the latter.

The valuable manuscript volume[1] of Rev. Thomas Shepard, from which several pages have been taken, was found quite difficult to decipher, some of it defying the skill of the most experienced expert, so that our copy is not entirely perfect; but perseverance has for the most part succeeded in penetrating its mysteries; in which effort we have been very kindly and materially aided, in the hardest places, by the suggestions of Mr. John W. Dean, one of the officers of the Historic-Genealogical Society, and of David Pulsifer, Esq.

The author is much indebted to Mr. Sibley, the courteous librarian of Harvard College, for permission to examine manuscripts relating to the subject of the memoir,

[1] Page 257.

and also, primarily, for the interesting account which we give of the discovery of Mr. Dunster's grave.

Much aid and encouragement have been afforded by two of President Dunster's direct descendants, Mr. Samuel Dunster, of Attleboro', Mass., and his son, Edward Swift Dunster, M.D., of New York, a graduate of Harvard in the year 1856. The genealogical table of the Dunster Family was prepared by them, with great care.

The author has spared no pains to make this volume a faithful portrait of the eminent person who forms its principal subject, and of the times during which he acted so conspicuous a part. He trusts that it may subserve the cause of Truth and Spiritual Freedom.

CONTENTS.

CHAPTER IX.

CHAPTER X.

CHAPTER XI.

CHAPTER XII.

CHAPTER XIII.

CHAPTER XIV.

CHAPTER XV.

CHAPTER XVI.

APPENDIX.

"I AM not the man you take me to be."

President Dunster's "Considerations," addressed to the General Court, 1654.

"I conceived then, and so do still, that I spake the truth in the feare of God, and dare not deny the same or go from it untill the Lord otherwise teach me; and this I pray the Honored Court to take for mine Answer."

From his Letter to the Middlesex County Court, 1655.

Life of Henry Dunster.

CHAPTER I.

IT may seem a late day to write the memoirs of a man's life, more than two hundred years after his death. But when that life evidently furnishes an example worthy of study and imitation in whatever period of the world, the long neglect to do it justice is only an additional reason for rescuing it from comparative oblivion, and lifting it, if so we may, to a merited prominence. Such, we believe, was the life of Henry Dunster, the first president of the first College in America.

Henry Dunster was a native of Lancashire, England, — " Ego enim Lancastrensis sum,"[1] is his own language, — and was one of that noble

[1] Page 272.

company, who, in the seventeenth century, emigrated to the New World, and laid the foundations of our civil and religious institutions.

The place and year of his birth cannot be exactly ascertained. Since the discovery, in the year 1852, of a letter[1] from his father written to him, from England, after his arrival in America, it has generally been believed that he was born in or near the town of Bury, as that letter is dated at Balehoult,[2] which is supposed to have been a gentleman's seat in the vicinity of Bury, and which appears to have been the family residence. Then there are extant two letters[3] from President Dunster to friends in and near Bury, of a character which seems to indicate the writer's intimate connection with the place. The question would be settled in favor of Bury, if we should accept the records of a Dunster family contained in the parish register of that town, as that of the family of the father of the President. There are strong points of correspondence, but discrepancies, also, which it is difficult, perhaps impossible, to reconcile. One difficulty in the way,

[1] Page 21 and IV. Mass. Hist. Collections II., 190, n.

[2] Page 256.

[3] Pages 276–288.

is the year (1620) assigned in the register for the baptism (and birth)[1] of the son Henry, which would make him but twenty years old when he arrived in New England and became President of the College. This, however, of itself, would not be an insuperable objection to the birth-date in the parish records. The average age of matriculation in the English universities in the seventeenth century was fourteen,[2] the age at which Jeremy Taylor entered College, and there is nothing unreasonable in supposing that Dunster may have entered a year younger, especially as he seems to have been a somewhat precocious youth. In that case, he could have received his first degree in 1637, and his second in 1640, the very year of his coming to New England. Not to mention other notable examples of very early development and promotion, in ancient and modern times, that of Cotton Mather is specially in point. This distinguished Puritan was graduated at Harvard College when he was fifteen, and

[1] Page 254.

[2] Mullinger. Cambridge in the Seventeenth Century. The present average is between eighteen and nineteen. On The Cam. By William Everett.

was settled in the old North Church, Boston, as his father's colleague, when twenty-one, having, at this early period of his life, earned an extraordinary reputation for scholarship. But the parish record does not agree with the dates of Mr. Dunster's obtaining his first and second degrees at the University, 1630 and 1634, as given by Savage.[1] Perhaps future researches in England may clear up these difficulties. At present, however, we must accept these last dates as correct. Assuming that Mr. Dunster went to Cambridge when he was fourteen, the year of his birth would be 1612, and he would be twenty-eight when he left England.

Mr. Dunster's father, also Henry, appears to have been a religious man, of the Puritan stamp. Besides Henry, we know that he had three sons, Thomas, mentioned in the father's letter alluded to above, as a widower, who had lost his wife and children, Richard and Robert; and at least three daughters, Elisabeth, Mary, and, according to Savage, but upon what authority we do not know, a third named Rose.[2] Richard,

1 Geneal. Dict. and Young's Chron. of Mass. 553, n.

2 Gen. Dict., Art. Hills.

who, we suppose, was younger than Henry, as he was commended by the father to his "good counsell," came to America, probably in his brother's company. The sisters remained with the parents — "wee two ould folke" — and the other brothers, but subsequently made New England their home, Elisabeth becoming the second, and Mary the third, wife of Major Simon Willard,[1] of Concord, a distinguished name in the early history of Massachusetts, and Rose, the wife of Captain Joseph Hills, of Malden, a gentleman of note, and Speaker of the General Court "in the earliest year."

As a child, Henry seems to have been thoughtful above his years. Even at the age of four or five, the religious awakening which stirred the Puritan element of England, arrested his attention. In the account of his Christian experience given to the Cambridge church in 1640, as preserved in manuscript notes by the pastor, Rev. Thomas Shepard,[2] speaking of that early period

1 "The Dunsters and Willards are intimately allied, having a common transmitted inheritance of blood flowing through the veins of very numerous descendants." Willard Memoir. By Joseph Willard.

2 Page 262.

of his life, he mentions a Mr. Hubbard, a "powerfull" and popular preacher, and says: "I heard many scoff at his preachinge, at this great flocking after him, and I asked why men did so. They said, to heare the word; and I said, then if it be the word, why do men speake against it; if it be not, why do men heare it?" Here appears even in the child that inquiring spirit and logical bent of mind which distinguished Mr. Dunster in later years.

When he was about twelve years old, he became deeply concerned as to his personal responsibility to God. "The Lord gave me," he relates, "an attentive eare and heart to understand preachinge. . . . The Lord showed me my sins, and reconciliation by Christ," "and this word was more sweet to me than any thing else in the world."

This was probably the commencement of that religious life which we shall see grandly developed in his subsequent career in New England. Not only when a boy at home, but in mature years, amid powerful temptations to sacrifice his convictions to personal advantages, the truth of God was "made more sweet to [him] than any thing else in the world."

But after that first experience of delight in religious things, he was destined to pass through years of inward conflict before he arrived at settled peace. "The greatest thing," he says, "which separated my soule from God was an inordinate desire of humane learning." But he wisely concluded to meet the temptation, and go to the University at Cambridge. He came out of the trial an humble and earnest Christian, not spoiled by learning and culture, but fitted thereby for the wide sphere of usefulness designed for him by Providence, in after years, in the New World.

From an early period, Cambridge University [1] had a special reputation for liberality of sentiment, which at one time went to a latitudinarian extreme, and hence it "fostered [Protestantism] towards the end of the sixteenth century, as it had promoted the Reformation fifty years before.

[1] "In the early state of the University the students lodged in hostels, or houses hired in the town [at their own expense]; but in process of time Colleges were founded and endowed by various benefactors for the promotion of piety and learning under a well-ordered system of internal discipline, and for affording assistance towards the maintenance of the inmates." Cooper. Memorials of Cambridge.

In 1565, the University was restive under the yoke of ceremonies, and almost all the men of St. John's came to chapel without hoods or surplices." "Sidney was Puritan, and so was Catharine Hall." "Cambridge had the credit of being 'a nest of Puritans' in the middle of King James' reign."[1] In this respect Emmanuel College was pre-eminent. This house was founded in 1585, in the twenty-seventh year of Elisabeth, by Sir Walter Mildmay, Chancellor of the Exchequer, "to be a nursery of Divines for the maintenance of the true Protestant religion against Popery and all other heresies whatsoever." The Queen is reported to have said to him, "So, Sir Walter, I hear that you have erected a Puritan foundation." "No, Madam," he replied, with a measure of courtier-like evasion, "far be it from me to countenance any thing contrary to your established laws; but I have set an acorn, which, when it becomes an oak, God alone knows what will be the fruit thereof." "The fruit," says Stoughton, "proved Puritan to the heart's core." And Fuller,[2] who relates the story, says of this College:

[1] Rev. J. Stoughton, D.D., Church of the Civil Wars, I. 474.

[2] History of the University of Cambridge.

"Sure I am at this day it hath overshadowed all the University." "During the period of the Commonwealth, no less than eleven heads of other Colleges in this University came from this house."[1] In Percy's Ballads, we find the following hit from Corbet's satirical poem (1615):

> "In the house of pure Emanuel
> I had my education,
> Where my friends surmise
> I dazzled my eyes
> With the light of Revelation.
> Boldly I preach, hate a cross, hate a surplice,
> Mitres, capes, and rotchets;
> Come hear me pray, nine times a day,
> And fill your heads with crotchets."

So many were the graduates of this University who came to New England, and helped to found or foster the new College, that it has been well said: "Cambridge in America is the child of Cambridge in England."[2]

New England was even more indebted than this to the English Cambridge, especially to Emmanuel College, — for from this house Higginson

[1] Cooper. Memorials of Cambridge. [2] On The Cam.

of Salem, Shepard of Cambridge, Hooker of New Haven, Harvard, who gave half his fortune, his library, and his name to the infant American College, John Cotton, Hugh Peter, Richard Saltonstall,[1] Simon Bradstreet, the last a Governor of Massachusetts, and many others came to New England to occupy important positions in its churches and commonwealths. John Robinson, father of the Pilgrim Colony, was a graduate of Emmanuel. Other Colleges of Cambridge gave such men to the New World as Wilson and Norton, of Boston, John Eliot, the apostle to the Indians, Charles Chauncy, the second President of Harvard College, and Roger Williams.[2]

Mr. Dunster was educated at Magdalen College, of which the quaint Thomas Fuller, the his-

[1] Richard, son of Sir Richard Saltonstall (217, n.) was a magistrate in the Massachusetts Colony, and, like his father, was a man of catholic views and tolerant spirit. Both were liberal benefactors of Harvard College. The son seems to have formed a warm attachment to Mr. Dunster. Writing to him from England in 1651, he addresses him as "my very worthy friend," "worthily endeared," and says, "I may truly tell you, you are written in my catalogue with greate letters."

[2] See Arnold's History of Rhode Island, I. 49. He took the degree of B.A., in Pembroke College, in 1626–7, the year that Mr. Dunster was matriculated at Magdalen.

torian of the University, says: "This college alone [of all the colleges that constitute the University] is on the northwest of the river, having the Rose-garden on the one, and what is no rose (a smoking brew house) on the other side thereof, belonging this 150 years to Jesus College. . . . Every year this house produces some eminent scholars, as living cheaper and privater, freer from town temptations by their remote situation."

According to the reckoning of Savage, Dunster was at Cambridge during at least two years of Dr. John Preston's mastership of Emmanuel College, and felt, as he himself informs us, the influence of his decided Puritan teachings. This divine, who succeeded Dr. Chadderton (a Puritan, and one of the translators of King James' Bible), as head of this College, was regarded by the Puritans of England as their leading man; and he not only "kept up the reputation of [his own College] as the most Puritanical in the University,"[1] but made his influence felt through the other houses, by his public lectures and sermons, especially as "Town-lecturer" at Trinity Church — an appointment which he received in 1623–4.

[1] Masson. Life and Times of Milton, I.

Mr. Dunster, afterwards alluding to his College days, says:[1] "After this I went to Cambridge, when, growing more careless, I lost my comfort. But I came to Trinity to hear Dr. Preston, by whom I was quickened and revived." Mr. Dunster also mentions "Mr. Goodwin" as one to whom he was much indebted for religious counsel during his College course. Thomas Goodwin, who "was, in many respects, the greatest divine among them all"[2] in the Westminster Assembly, was lecturer at Trinity before Dr. Preston, and was afterwards made President of Magdalen College by Oliver Cromwell.

Among the contemporaries of Dunster at the University, for at least a part of his course, were Ralph Cudworth, author of *The True Intellectual System of the Universe*, Henry More, the Platonist, Joseph Mede, a learned commentator on the Apocalypse, John Pearson, afterwards a bishop, and expositor of the Creed, Jeremy Taylor and John Milton; the last of whom was two years in advance of Dunster, but, as he remained three years after his graduation, studying for his second degree, the two may have spent four years

[1] Page 263. [2] Stoughton.

together at the University. It is not unlikely, also, that Dunster prosecuted, as a resident graduate, those Oriental studies which gained him a high reputation even before he left his native land. It is worthy of note, that John Harvard, who was afterwards a generous benefactor of the New-England Cambridge, spent more than two years of his University course with one who became its first President, the former having entered Emmanuel College in 1628, the latter, Magdalen College, in 1626.

Cotton Mather speaks of Mr. Dunster as having exercised his ministry in England. It is probable that, like most of the early Puritan ministers of New England, he had taken orders in the Established Church, and that he retained that connection till after his arrival in the New World. In his Confession of Faith,[1] he says: "The Lord hath made me bid adieu to all worldly treasures; and, as corruptions in the Church came, first I began to suspect them, then to hate them." To which he adds: "So, after 10 years' trouble, I came hither [to New England]; and the Lord gives me peace to see the order of his people."

[1] Page 265.

In two letters[1] of his, which have been preserved, written from New England, one to Mr. Alt, a Church of England minister, at Bury, and the other to "Christian friends in and about Bury," Mr. Dunster forcibly argues the right of separation from a corrupt church for the purpose of forming, or uniting with, a purer body. These letters would appear to be in part a vindication of his own conduct and that of his New England brethren, in seceding from the Episcopal Church. Referring to Mr. Alt's arguments, in reply probably to a letter from him, Mr. Dunster says: "It's a glorious church, say you. Whence, I pray you, was it gathered, out of the Church of Rome, or else yet it stands in it? If it stand yet in it, then it is one of the daughters of the great whore, pudet haec opprobria nobis, et dici potuisse refelli. No; the Church of England is gathered out of Rome. Come out of her, my people. Go to then, behold a church gathered out of a church. . . . But why should we gather a church out of the English Church? I pray you, Sir, where hath Christ constituted a church of that form? Where's the national ministry, temple

[1] Pages 276–280.

&c.? If you will find this, you have the verity, we the vanity. If congregations be the visible churches of Christ, we have the day in that respect."

In the other letter, addressed, we infer, to friends, some in, and some separated from, the Church of England, he says: "If any that utter big and bitter invectives against the Congregational way, can convince any members of the same that they have separated themselves from the saints and people of God, that they may live profanely, unrighteously, luxuriantly and wantonly &c., or to any other end that is contrary to sound doctrine, I think they shall do well to admonish them by the Word of the Lord, which they have transgressed. But if they have only withdrawn themselves from [the] communion of, and communicating with, the dark, profane and scandalous world, that lieth in that Evil One, 1 John v. 19; that knoweth not Christ, nor hath received his Spirit, that they may live together in holy communion with Christ and his people in all his instituted ordinances, then I say, whosoever condemn these people, Christ's word will justify them to and before all his true churches in the world. And his Spirit will speak peace to their spirits whoever have so done in sincerity, as unto sons and daughters of the Living God. Glorious, I confess, and forever honorable to those instruments of Christ, is that passage in the 33d page of the Vindication of the Army's Declaration against the Scots' Reply: 'Give us leave to ask you of Scotland, who alone would seem to be the true Reformers, whether we have any [n]ational sins, as the compulsive joining of the precious with the vile in the administration of the seals of the covenant of grace, or the corrupt and horrible constitution of the matter of your churches, making them up of people grossly ignorant and very scandalous &c.'"

Yet with all this Puritanic strictness, his noble charity shines out in the following passage from this same letter: "Yet truly all your letters speak such plain and candid expressions of your single, sincere hearts, that, for my part, I can, with every good assurance in my own heart, believe Christ Jesus hath gathered you all in one and the same church mystical and spiritual, even into that body whereof he is the head, in whom, if you lovingly strive together in faith and love, then for outward administrations bear kindly one with another, where you cannot by the Word of the Lord clearly convince your brother of sin."

From Mr. Dunster's "Christian Experience" we learn that after leaving the University, he spent some time, probably before engaging, or fully so, in the ministry, in teaching school.[1]

[1] Page 263.

CHAPTER II.

THOSE were troublous times, and big with great events, when Mr. Dunster left England. Charles I. with Strafford as lord-lieutenant and archbishop Laud as chief-inquisitor, was seeking to compel uniformity to the Established Church, in its semi-popish character. Then flourished the Council Table, Star Chamber and High Commission, infamous engines for crushing out the liberties of England. Non-conforming Protestants were the victims of intolerable oppression, so that in twelve years of Laud's administration four thousand persons emigrated to America, among whom were many eminent Puritan divines. "The sun," said they, "shines as pleasantly on America as on England, and the Sun of Righteousness much more clearly. The Church of England has added to the ceremonies and habits of Popery the only marks of

Antichrist which were wanting, corruption of doctrine and serious persecution of her members. Let us move whither the Providence of God calls, and make that our country which will afford us what is dearer to us than our property or our lives, the liberty of worshipping God in a way which appears to us most conducive to our eternal welfare."

It had been the plan of Elizabeth to get rid of Puritanism by expelling dissentients from the kingdom, but another policy was adopted by Charles, who issued a proclamation forbidding emigration to New England except by special license; and, because "such ministers as are not conformable to the discipline and ceremonies of the Church do frequently transport themselves to the plantations, where they take liberty to nourish their factious and schismatical humours," it was ordered, that no clergyman should be suffered to go without a testimonial from the archbishop of Canterbury, and the bishop of London. "The people of New England," said the king, "are factious and unworthy of our support."

But in spite of these orders, not a few nonconformists escaped to the New World; though the emigration in 1639 and 1640 was very much below that of previous years.

The letter alluded to above, written to Mr. Dunster from his father,* and fortunately rescued from oblivion "after it had long been given up for lost," refers to various events which had recently taken place in the mother country, and which were the prelude to the Civil War that overthrew the monarchy and established the Puritan Commonwealth. The attempt of Charles to impose Episcopacy upon the Scotch had roused them to an armed resistance, which led to the invasion of England and the possession of the town of Newcastle, in the year 1640, followed in November of the same year, by the assembling of the Long Parliament, the impeachment and

* In the year 1852, this interesting document was presented by Miss Hannah Dunster, of Pembroke, Mass., a daughter of Rev. Isaiah Dunster, of Harwich, Mass., great-grandson of the president, to Edward S. Dunster, then a student in Harvard College. Miss Dunster was then 84 years of age. The letter was copied by Rev. Samuel Sewall, of Burlington, Mass., a connection of the family by marriage, and, with other "Dunster Papers," was published in the Massachusetts Histor. Collections (IV. series, vol. ii.). The original, with other papers and relics of President Dunster, is now in the possession of Mr. Samuel Dunster of Attleboro', Mass.

execution of Laud and Strafford and the beheading of the king. It was this same year that Oliver Cromwell, then forty years of age, was elected to Parliament from Cambridge. The Prince of Wales, afterwards Charles II., was then ten years old.

LETTER.

Grace, mercy and peace be multiplied in Christ Jesus upon you. Amen.

Kind and loving sons, I am very glad of your welfare and good prosperity. I have received four letters from you since you arrived in New England, the first dated the 17th of August, by Robert Haworth, of Boulton, the second dated the 21st of August, both which came to my hand in seven weeks after you sent them. The red wheat I received, but the Indian wampem pegs[1] were lost out of your letter. The third was dated the 29th of October, which I received on Christmas eve, with a letter of Richard's enclosed in the same; the last dated the 12th of

[1] Wampum peaque — Indian money, then and long after current among the English. To the time of the American Revolution of 1775, a peag or peaque was valued as the sixth part of a penny. Drake. Hist. of Boston.

October, which I received of one Millus, that had been with you in New England, who lodged with me about mid January, but it seems it should have come by Colier. Your sisters remember their loves unto you both, but you must not expect them so long as your mother and I do live.[1] Your brother Thomas remembers his love, and hath sent you two dozen of almanacks ; but now he is a widower, for both wife and children are dead since Michaelmas. I pray God he take good ways. I do not know of any that you sent for that entend to come as yet. Touching Richard, I would advise him not to come over again as yet, for whatsoever is his due shall be left in the hands of his sisters, for I have taken a general acquittance of Robert, so that Richard and his sisters may have what we two old folk leave, and we will make no waste. Now concerning our England, since you went over we have been sore troubled, for the Scotts came into England

[1] Willard (Willard Memoir, p. 363, n.) supposes that the parents must have died soon after the date of this letter, and that Elisabeth (and probably another sister) left England immediately after their death, reaching New England as early as May, 1641.

a month fore Michaelmas, and came to Tyne water, where some of our troopers lay. The Scotts proffered to come over, and our men withstood them for a while, but ours being but 500 were not able to withstand thirty thousand, but fled amain, insomuch as one Constable, a gentleman of a company, cried to his band, Ride, thieves, ride for your lives: and he himself, for his part, rode so fast that he lost his cap, and missed it not of riding two miles. Then the Scotts came pedentim towards Newcastle in some 2 or 3 days, where they yielded the town immediately. Then was England in a fright, for they did not know what to do. But at last all the freeholders and trained band were called together, every hundred by itself, and trained for a fortnight together, so that upon the eighth of September, being Bury Fair, there was at Bury 40 thousand with such weapons as they could get, and those that had no better, took everyone a great club, and it was called club fair at Bury, and all the provision for the fair was eaten up that day, so that the 800 which trained there were scanted for a fortnight after of victuals. The butchers and alewives[1] made a gain of them.

[1] Women who kept alehouses.

Then great troops of soldiers were sent into Yorkshire, and it was thought that there would have been some battle speedily, but the Lord turned all to peace, and a Parliament[1] was called, which began the 3d of November, and they go on very joyfully. God be praised for the same. And the Scotts are to remove from Newcastle before the 25th of March, and they must receive 300 thousand pounds to bring them home again. Now for our great men of England, the most of them are proved traitors. First, Lord Deputy of Ireland[2] and the archbishop of Canterbury[3] and the great Judges. The rest of the bishops are found in a premunire[4] except the bishop of

[1] The Long Parliament. [2] Strafford. [3] Laud.

[4] In order to prevent the pope from assuming the supremacy in granting ecclesiastical livings, a number of statutes were made in England during the reign of Edward I., and his successors, punishing certain acts of submission to the papal authority. In the writ for the execution of these statutes, the words *praemunire facias*, being used to command a citation of the party, gave not only to the writ, but to the offence itself, of maintaining the papal power, the name of *praemunire*. Bouvier. Law Dictionary.

The Puritan party, when in the ascendant, availed themselves of these statutes against the adherents of Charles and the Church party.

Lincoln,[1] who is supposed to be in the Parliament house. All the rest are excluded. Finch, the lord-keeper, is fled. Wyndebanck, the king's [2] chief secretary, is fled. The bishop Wren [3] had thought to have flown, but his wings were too short. All non-conformists are suffered to preach, and our altars are some of them pulled up, surplice and communion books some torn, the communion-tables brought down into the body of the church. Burton and Prynne [4] are

[1] Dr. John Williams. [2] Charles I.

[3] Wren, bishop of Norwich, had been chaplain to Charles I. Being suspected of treason by the parliamentary party, he was thrown into prison during the period of the Civil War, where he lay eighteen years. Under Charles II. he regained his bishoprick.

[4] Henry Burton, a Puritan clergyman, strongly opposed the proceedings of Laud. For preaching what were regarded as seditious sermons, he was, in 1637, condemned by the Star Chamber to a fine of £5,000, to have his ears cut off, and to be imprisoned. In 1640, the Long Parliament restored him to liberty and his "living."

William Prynne, a lawyer, also rendered himself obnoxious to Laud, and was sentenced to the pillory, a heavy fine, the loss of his ears, to be branded on the forehead, and imprisoned for life. The year 1640 brought his release, and a place in the parliament. Both of these men were "escorted into London by a calvacade of 5,000 men and women decked with rosemary and bags." See May's History of the Long Parliament.

brought into the parliament-house with great respect, and were met out of the city with 200 coaches in triumph, so that the king did take it somewhat harshly, and said so many did not meet him when he came from York from quieting the Scotts. Many petitions are proffered into the Parliament against idle, drunken ministers and against double beneficed parsons, and suit made that all chapels shall be relieved out of church livings. Your sister Elisabeth is turned scribe, and can do very well of three weeks' time. I pray you give Richard good counsel, and be the means to train him up in goodness, and make much of each other, for it repenteth me very sore of my life heretofore spent in idle company, and I thank God heartily, that prolonged my life to see my errors and folly.

The old lady Ashton and Mr. Rawsthorns have died within two hours together upon Wednesday afore Candlemas, and were buried at Bury both in one grave upon the Monday following. The papists had conspired with the Deputy of Ireland[1] to set fighting in the north parts that

[1] Strafford.

they might have begun in the South where they should have had aid out of Ireland, and the Spaniard lay watching upon the seas likewise to have aided them, but the Hollanders meeting with them, gave them a great stroke and scattered them sore, so that we may well say, that men purposseth but God disposeth. My Lord Saye and my Lord Brooke[1] are sworn of the king's privy counsel, whose lives the bishops had meant to have taken away. Not long since your old friend Doctor Cossins for his honesty is put in the cage to see if he can sing well or no. All the monopolies for licenses are disannulled, so that every man may buy and sell at their pleasure without control. We have gotten old Mr. Horocks to be lecturer at Bury every Thursday. He began afore Christmas, and hath promised for a twelvemonth, if God spare his health and ability. Mr. Ashton of Middleton is one of the knights for the Parliament, who hath with him

[1] Lord Say and Sele and Lord Brook were both of them distinguished for worth of character, and were deeply interested in the settlement of New England. At one time they proposed to emigrate to America. At the restoration, under Charles II., Lord Say became Keeper of the Privy Seal.

for advise and counsel your friend old Mr. Rathband, who hath been with him since it began.

The Scotts, as soon as they came to Newcastle, sang the 74th psalm: 'Why art thou, Lord, so long from us,'[1] &c. Many great men are thought to be faulty, as I writ afore. Thus committing you both to the protection of the Almighty, I rest,

Your loving father,

HENRYE DUNSTER.

From Balehout this 20th of March, 1640 [1640-1].[2]

The writer was evidently in warm sympathy with the party which aimed at the most thorough reformation in civil and religious affairs. His son Henry was of the same mind. He was opposed to Charles, the monarchy, and the national Church, and to the Presbyterian party,

[1] Sternhold and Hopkins' version.

[2] According to "Old Style," which continued in use in New England till the year 1752, the year began in March. To prevent any doubt whether January, February and a part of March ended the old year or began the new, it was customary to date as in the text — "20th of March, 1640-1." There is no difference as to the year between the two Styles, after the 25th of March.

which sought to establish a national Church, after the Scottish pattern, as indeed it actually did for a brief period. "A reformation of the Scottish edition," wrote Mr. Dunster,[1] some time after his arrival in America, "it [will] leave you in deep distress, inward and outward." "National and provincial churches are nullities *in rerum natura*, since the dissolution of that of the Jews." "For the monarchy, man's wickedness as the meritorious cause, and God's providence and mighty hand as the efficient cause hath dissolved [it]. The nation then is free from it. . . . No man's oath tieth him to what is not. If the people and nation be free from monarchy, the question is, what form they should set up? And what, I pray you, but that which is most suitable to the matter? I say, to the form which is most suitable to the matter; which the nation itself by their faithful representatives, being pious and prudent men, can best judge of."

Here the republican doctrine of the right of the people to choose their own form of government and their own rulers, is clearly stated. Whether he had yet rid himself of the doctrine,

[1] Page 286.

which most unfortunately and inconsistently then characterized the Puritans of Old and New England, that the civil arm was bound to support the church, we have no means of knowing. If he accepted this opinion, such a liberal mind as his could not long retain it. In religious matters, he certainly recognized the supremacy of Jesus Christ, as head of the church, against all human authority. Referring to certain sermons preached by Mr. Shepard, he said: "But I list not to stay to justify any phrases of men. That vanity (blessed be the Lord) is well blasted, of human authority in the church of Christ, where this canon is received, [viz.] 'This is my beloved Son, hear him,' whom the Father hath sent to be head of the church. To whom who will not hearken, the Lord require it of them."[1] The subsequent career of one so catholic and progressive in his spirit need not be a matter of surprise. How could he do otherwise than claim for himself and all others, the Quakers, for instance, the right of private judgment?

[1] Page 278.

CHAPTER III.

MR. DUNSTER arrived in Boston "toward the latter end of this summer,"[1] that of 1640. For a short time, he resided in Boston, "on his own estate, at the North East corner of Court Street and Washington Street."[2]

Boston, now a city of 240,000 inhabitants, was then only a village, the peninsula on which it was originally built comprising but 700 acres. In 1634, Wood, in his Description of Massachusetts, gave this record of his impressions of the place: Its "situation is very pleasant, being a peninsula hemmed in on the South side with the bay of Roxberry, on the North side with Charles River, the marshes on the back side being not half of a quarter of a mile over; so that a little fencing will secure the cattle from the wolves. It being a neck, and bare of wood, they are not troubled

1 Wonder-Working Providence, p. 162. 2 Whitman.

with three great annoyances, of wolves, rattlesnakes and mosquitoes." In 1638, it was said to be "rather a village than a town, consisting of no more than twenty or thirty houses." Thirty-five years after Mr. Dunster's arrival, it had 4,000 inhabitants.

In 1643, in the four Confederated Colonies,[1] there was a population of about 24,000, of whom 15,000 were in Massachusetts, 3,000 each in Plymouth and Connecticut, and 2,500 in New Haven.[2] In Massachusetts there were twenty-six towns, and 1,708 persons entitled to the franchise; which agrees with the statement of Lechford, in 1640, that about one fourth of the people of Massachusetts were at that time in the church, less than one eighth therefore having the privileges of freemen.

[1] In 1643, these Colonies formed a league "for mutual help and strength," under the name of "The United Colonies of New England." Two Commissioners were to be chosen from each of the Colonies, to meet annually either at Boston, Hartford, New Haven, or Plymouth. This Confederation was a sort of Congress, though for the most part only advisory. It lasted forty-one years. Rhode Island, for obvious reasons, was not allowed a place in the Confederacy.

[2] Palfrey. Hist. of N. England, I.

In 1640, there were twenty-nine churches in Massachusetts and Plymouth, to which fifteen more were added during the next ten years.

Though Boston at that time was numerically an inconsiderable place, yet it had an enterprising population. About this period, chiefly through the influence of the famous Hugh Peter, six large vessels were built, and a commerce was carried on not only with the mother country, but with Madeira, the Canaries, Spain &c., staves, and codfish being exchanged for wines, sugar, and dried fruit.[1] Hemp and flax were already cultivated, and the manufacture of linen, woollen and cotton cloths had been commenced in the Colony.

In 1640, there was but a solitary lawyer in Massachusetts, probably in all New England,[2] Thomas Lechford of Lincoln's Inn, who had

[1] Hildreth. Hist. of the United States, I.

[2] The General Court, in 1639, took Mr. Lechford in hand "for going to a jewry and pleading with them out of Court;" for which he was "debarred from pleading any man's cause hereafter, unless his owne, and admonished not to presume to meddle beyond what he shall be called to by the Court." A little after, having "acknowledged [such is the Court record] he had overshot himself, and was sorry for it, promising to attend his calling,

come to try his fortune in Boston ; and so extreme was the prejudice against his profession, that after an uncomfortable residence of three years among an unappreciating people, he returned, in the year 1641, in disgust, to his native England, where lawyers were more respected. What was said by John Rogers, a graduate of Harvard College under Mr. Dunster, and its President in 1683, about the "incredible wickedness of that profession," expressed the opinion prevalent among our Puritan fathers. As late as

and not to meddle with controversies," he "was dismissed." Mass. Col. Records, I. 270, 310.

In the Plymouth Colony there were no lawyers for many years. For a time the General Court was the only Court, and the Governor and Assistants tried most of the cases during the whole history of the Colony. They discarded all the cumbersome forms in use at that time in England, and adopted such forms as their own good sense dictated. Punishments were often left to the discretion of the Court. For some years their deeds of lands were neither signed nor sealed ; but an acknowledgment of the sale was made before a magistrate, who made a memorandum of it. It was not till 1671 that the law expressly authorized any party to employ one or two attorneys on his case, but on the express condition that they should do nothing "to deceive the Court, or to darken the case." The Colony of New Plymouth &c. William Brigham.

1687, fifty-nine years after the settlement of Boston, that town, and probably the Colony, had but two lawyers. Had it been revealed to our pious ancestors, that, two hundred years later, in Boston alone, the two should be multiplied to eight hundred, they would have proclaimed a fast and arrayed themselves in sackcloth, in view of the coming calamity.

But what the society of Boston and vicinity lacked in gentlemen of the bar, it more than made up in able and learned ministers. In 1640, over the one church of Boston were two eminent preachers, John Cotton,[1] then fifty-five, and

[1] Cotton had been a pastor in Boston, England, before coming to Boston in New England. "Its ancient church of St. Botolph was," says Palfrey, "perhaps the most stately parish church in England, a cathedral in size and beauty. It was from this superb temple that John Cotton came to preach the gospel within the mud walls and under the thatched roof of the meeting house in a rude New England hamlet." Hist. N. E. I. 368.

Hubbard, a graduate of Harvard College, in 1642, and author of a History of New England down to 1680, says of Mr. Cotton, that "he had such an insinuating and melting way in his preaching that he would usually carry his very adversary captive after the triumphant chariot of his rhetoric." He was called the "father of Congregationalism," and was more influential than any other man, in establishing the New England theocracy.

John Wilson fifty-two, both Cambridge graduates, and "the most powerful of [the] ecclesiastical leaders" of New England; the former, according to the custom of that day, the Teacher of the church, the other its Pastor, a distinction doubtless quite without a difference. Thomas Shepard,[1] "a poore, weake, pale-complectioned man," but a "gratious, sweete, heavenly-minded, and soul-ravishing minister," then thirty-five, was settled at Cambridge. The future "apostle to the Indians," John Eliot, at the age of thirty-six, was pastor at Roxbury, and already forecasting his work among the natives of the forest. Richard Mather, from Oxford, the father of Increase Mather, afterward President of the College, and grandfather of Cotton Mather — himself to be, a few years later, the principal author of the Cambridge Platform, the authoritative creed of the churches, was now, at the age of forty-four, pastor

1 Thomas Fuller (Hist. Cambridge University, Eng.) classes Shepard among "the learned writers of Emmanuel College." His works were greatly esteemed by President Edwards, who styled him "that famous experimental divine." He died at the age of 44. John Quincy Adams was a descendant in the sixth generation from Mr. Shepard. Young's Chron. of Mass. p. 558, note.

at Dorchester. John Norton, at the age of thirty-four was preaching in Ipswich, awaiting his transfer to Boston ; a strong preacher, but of a "melancholy temperament" and an intolerant spirit. The same town was also the abode of Nathaniel Ward, formerly a lawyer, now a preacher, author of that humorous but abusive work against religious toleration, *The Simple Cobbler of Agawam*, and of the *Body of Liberties*, the basis of Massachusetts legislation in its early days. Nearer, in Salem, was that singular man, Hugh Peter, preacher, politician, and political-economist, "the father of New England commerce, and the founder of her fisheries." At the same place was Edward Norris, a man of very different stamp, devoted to his pastoral work, of "distinguished learning and influence," and specially to be remembered for that tolerant spirit, alas, so rare in his day, which kept him from taking part in the proceedings against the Baptists. To these we might add other influential names.

Thus Mr. Dunster found himself in the midst of a circle of cultivated men, trained in the English Universities, who had come to the western wilderness to found a religious Commonwealth.

"There were probably at that time forty or fifty sons of the [English] University of Cambridge — one for every two hundred or two hundred and fifty inhabitants — dwelling in the few villages of Massachusetts and Connecticut. The sons of Oxford were not few."[1] Governor Hutchinson[2] says, "The reputation of the New England clergy had been for some time very great in England, and the opinions of Mr. Cotton, Mr. Hooker, Mr. Davenport and others, are cited as authorities by many English divines." Nathaniel Mather,[3] a brother of Increase, who, after his graduation at Harvard College, went to England to reside, wrote as follows, about the year 1650: "'Tis incredible what an advantage to preferment it is to have been a New Englishman."

One man, in some respects of congenial spirit with Dunster, was not now in Massachusetts. Four years before, Roger Williams, a graduate of Cambridge, had been banished into the wilderness, and was now, at the age of forty-one, building up his little republic at Providence, upon

[1] Savage. Note to Winthrop's Journal, 265.

[2] History of Massachusetts.

[3] IV. Hist. Col. viii. 3.

the sacred principle, avowed anew this very year, of "holding forth liberty of conscience."

But another great man, between whom and Williams there subsisted a friendship which the banishment of the latter could not sunder, and who, in his later years, regretted the part he had taken against the religious rights of his fellow-Christians of another name, contrary to the better instincts of his nature, — John Winthrop,[1] first governor of Massachusetts, was still living, at the age of fifty-four. Thomas Dudley was that year (1640) chosen Governor, and Richard Bellingham, Deputy Governor, able men, but severe towards dissenters from the established church. Endicott and Bradstreet, afterwards chief magistrates, and also stern toward "heretics," were now in the Colony.

[1] Hutchinson (Hist. of Massachusetts I. 142) says, "that upon his [Winthrop's] death bed, when Mr. Dudley pressed him to sign an order of banishment of an heterodox person, he refused, saying, '*I have done too much of that work already.*'"

In a letter to John Winthrop Jr., the accomplished son of the Governor of Massachusetts, Roger Williams shows the characteristic magnanimity of his nature, when he says that he "ever honored and loved and ever shall the root and branches of your deare name." Hist. Col. Winthrop Papers.

It was of these and such as these that Chalmers wrote as follows: "The principal planters of Massachusetts were English country gentlemen of no inconsiderable fortunes; of enlarged understandings, improved by liberal education."

In the sister Colony of the Pilgrims, "Elder" Brewster, a patient and loving spirit, was still living, at the age of fourscore; Bradford was Governor; and Prince and Winslow, Cudwor h and Hatherly, the last two noble champions of religious freedom, Miles Standish, the valorous captain, and John Alden, his traditional rival, were now among the leading men of that part of New England. In Connecticut, Edward Hopkins,[1] who afterwards, having returned to England to take part in the great contest for freedom, became member of Parliament, and Com-

[1] Quincy (I. 168) speaks of him as one of the noblest benefactors of the College, and as a "lofty and intellectual spirit." In his will, he left a thousand pounds to institutions in Connecticut, for the promotion of religion, science or charity, and five hundred pounds for the benefit of Harvard College, or its vicinity. "After an unceasing flow of annual benefits for more than a century, his bounty now exists on a foundation of productive and well-secured capital, amounting nearly to thirtv thousand dollars."

missioner for the Navy and Admiralty, was now Governor, and John Haynes,[1] five years before Governor of Massachusetts, was Deputy Governor. We refer to these prominent men in the different Colonies, as persons with whom Mr. Dunster was now for a series of years to come in contact, either socially, or as President of the only College in New England.

At this time there were probably about 50,000 Indians within the limits of New England, a few thousands of whom were in Massachusetts; some, as the friendly tribe at Newtown and Natick, in the close vicinity of the whites, while others, more remote, were threatening the peace of the Colony. This very year, 1640, Miantonomo, the great Narragansett chief, afterwards condemned to an unhappy fate which he did not deserve, came to Boston to talk with the Governor.

The great Antinomian controversy, in which Mrs. Anne Hutchinson was the central figure, had been terminated three years before by her banishment, and peace restored to the churches.

Another trouble to our Puritan fathers was

1 "A gentleman of large estate in England." Arnold.

now beginning to loom up, — the "Anabaptist" heresy, as it was deemed. Among the first settlers, according to Cotton Mather, there were persons holding anabaptist sentiments, but they had given little trouble to the Puritan churches. Now, however, the distemper was beginning to assume a more alarming aspect, and to attract the special attention of the guardians of the established religion. In 1640, Lady Deborah Moody, a person of noble family and of heroic character, whom Winthrop[1] styled "an anciently religious woman," came to Massachusetts, and united with the church at Salem; but the same year, she, with several others, became infected with the anabaptist doctrine. Being, three years after, excommunicated, she found it convenient to emigrate to Long Island, where she was disappointed in not finding a more tolerant government than she had fled from. Other indications of the spread of this heresy created much uneasiness.

We have stated that Mr. Dunster, for a short time, after his arrival, resided in Boston. It is somewhat singular that the name Dunster, just

[1] Journal.

at that time, appears on the roll of members of the Boston Artillery Company, now The Ancient and Honorable Artillery Company, which was formed in 1639 — the oldest regular military organization in America. The historian of the Company [1] has prefixed Henry to the surname, which is probably correct. It is certain that at that day the most religious men did not deem it unbecoming their sacred profession to take an active part in military affairs. It is stated that Rev. Mr. Cotton, of Boston,[2] was so much impressed with the importance of a strong military force, that he gave a thousand pounds for the purchase of cannon. Indeed, under the circumstances of the times, such a course was a necessity. The field exercises were opened and closed by prayer. Robert Keayne, "an ancient professor of the gospel," was the first captain of the above Company. Captain Johnson, author of *Wonder-Working Providence,* and very zealous in religious matters, was a member, at this time. "See," said he, "that with all diligence you encourage every soldier-like spirit among you, for the Lord Christ intends to achieve greater mat-

[1] Whitman. [2] Dearborn. Boston Notions.

ters by this little handful than the world is aware of." Another member, also in fellowship with the church in Boston, was Nicolas Upsal,[1] the brave man, who, afterwards, in 1656, then sixty years of age, when the cruel law enacted that year by the General Court against the Quakers, was proclaimed with beat of drum through the streets of Boston, came forth from his house, and openly warned the government, "that the execution of this law would be the forerunner of judgments on the land," beseeching them to beware what they did, "lest they might be found among those who were fighting against God" — a manly, Christian protest, which brought upon him swift punishment in the shape of a fine of twenty pounds and banishment from the Colony.

[1] Uhden's New England Theocracy, translated by Mrs. H. C. Conant.

CHAPTER IV.

MR. DUNSTER'S residence in Boston was very brief, for in August of the same year, which must have been almost immediately upon his arrival,[1] he was called by the elders, ministers and magistrates, almost by "acclamation," to remove to Cambridge, to engage in what proved to be his great life-work, as President of the College. The work was an arduous one, but it was doubtless congenial with his scholarly tastes, as well as answerable to his more sacred ambition to be useful in the kingdom of Christ; and he entered upon his task as a work of love and duty. The circumstances under which he undertook it must have seemed to him as the finger of Providence, and have made him feel that he had been led here for a high purpose, welcomed so cordially, as he was, by the leading men of the Colony, in

[1] Chap. III. page 31.

Church and State, and conducted immediately to a post, just made vacant, which all regarded as one of peculiar responsibility and dignity.

It is the testimony of his contemporaries, which later writers have unanimously indorsed, that Mr. Dunster brought to his work qualifications of no ordinary character. He was a profound scholar, especially in the Oriental languages, and an attractive preacher, and seemed to happily combine, as we gather from his subsequent career, decision of character with suavity of disposition. He was not a literary recluse, but put himself in sympathy with the great enterprise which had brought so many others to New England, the building up a Christian commonwealth. The men of that period were inspired by a noble enthusiasm, and Mr. Dunster was one with them in spirit, only that he proved himself to be in one great respect far superior to the majority of his contemporaries. Captain Johnson gave the opinion generally entertained of him, when in quaint prose and execrable poetry he said, at a little later period: "Mr. Henry Dunster is now President of this Colledge, fitted from the Lord for the work, and by those that have skill that way, reported to be an able Proficient in both Hebrew, Greek and Latine languages, an Orthodox Preacher of the truths of Christ, very powerful through his blessing to move the affections. . . . But seeing the Lord hath been pleased to raise up so worthy an instrument for their good, he shall not want for incouragement to go on with the work, so far as a rusticall rime shall reach.

Could man presage prodigious works at hand,
  Provide he would for's good and ill prevent,
But God both time and means hath at's command,
  Dunster in time to his New England hath sent.
When England 'gan to keep at home their guides,
  New England began to pay their borrowed back,[1]
Industrious Dunster, Providence provides,
  Our friends supply, and yet ourselves no lack.[2]"

Rev. Thomas Shepard, pastor at Cambridge during the first nine years of Mr. Dunster's administration, speaks of him as "a man pious, painful, and fit to teach, and very fit to lay the foundations of the domesticall affairs of the Col-

[1] Alluding to gentlemen in England having sent their sons to New England to be educated at Cambridge.

[2] Wonder-Working Providence.

lege; whom God hath much honored and blessed."[1] The following passage in a letter from Mr. Shepard to John Winthrop shows in what esteem he held Mr. Dunster's judgment and learning: "Your apprehensions agaynst reading and learning heathen authors, I perswade myselfe were suddenly suggested, and will easily be answered by H. Dunstar, if you should impart them to him."[2]

One of his successors in office, also an historian of the College, Josiah Quincy, well expresses the sentiment of our day, when he says: "Among the early friends of the College, no one deserves more distinct notice than Henry Dunster. He united in himself the character of both patron and President; for, poor as he was, he contributed, at a time of its utmost need, one hundred acres of land [in Shawsin, now Billerica] towards its support; besides rendering to it, for a succession of years, a series of official services, well directed, unwearied, and altogether inestimable."[3] Again he speaks of him as having "never omit-

[1] Mem. &c. Young's Chronicles of Mass. 552.

[2] IV. Hist. Col. VII.

[3] Hist. Harvard University, I.

ted any opportunity to be useful to the College," and as having "possessed a gentle heart and a noble vein of Christian charity." With reference to Dunster and his successor Chauncy, he says: "Both were able, faithful and earnest. . . . Both were learned beyond the measure of their contemporaries; and probably, in this respect, were surpassed by no one who has since succeeded to their chair." "President Dunster," says Peirce, an earlier historian of the College, "was a truly worthy, as well as an eminently learned man." Palfrey speaks of him as "the learned and excellent Mr. Dunster," of "eminent worth and accomplishments," under whose administration "a new era was inaugurated."

Such was the man who undertook the task of laying the foundations and moulding the character of the first College[1] on the American continent.

It was now only four years since the incipient steps were taken in the General Court, by the appropriation of four hundred pounds, towards establishing an institution of learning. Says the

[1] William and Mary College, Va., was founded fifty years later; Yale in 1701.

author of *New England's First Fruits,* published in 1643: "After God had carried us safe to New England, and we had builded our houses, provided necessaries for our livelihood, reared convenient places for God's worship, and settled the civil government; one of the next things we longed for and looked after was to advance learning and perpetuate it to posterity; dreading to leave an illiterate ministery to the Churches when our present ministers shall lie in the dust."[1] The College Seal, *In Christi Gloriam,* and the later one which was substituted for it, *Christo et Ecclesiæ,*[2] show the spirit and main design of the

1 About the year 1652, the Second Church in Boston, having failed to secure a pastor, called Mr. Powell, one of their own number, to conduct their worship. His services were so acceptable, that they would have ordained him as their Teacher, had not the General Court objected that he was "illiterate as to academical education," and was therefore specially unfit "in such a place as Boston." "If," they argued, "such men intrude themselves into the sacred function, there is danger of bringing the profession into contempt. If an exception should be made in the case of Mr. Powell, by reason of his peculiar gifts, it might establish a dangerous precedent." Mass. Hist. Coll. Robbins' History of the Second Church.

2 In this connection the following sentiments uttered by President Stearns of Amherst College, and Hon. John H. Clifford,

founders and friends of the College. It was to be a "School of the Prophets," while at the same time it was to promote the general interests of learning.

The selection of Cambridge as the site of the College, was not only because it was "a place

President of the Board of Overseers of Harvard College, will be read with interest:

"Our old colleges were founded for Christian education, manhood and usefulness. Even the mottoes and devices of the college seals bear witness to the fact. The first and temporary seal of Harvard contained three open Bibles, with a syllable of the word *Veritas* upon each of them; its second temporary seal, the same three Bibles, with the words *In Christi gloriam:* the words which characterize its permanent and present seal are *Christo et Ecclesiæ.* Yale has one open Bible, with the Hebrew words of the high priest's breastplate, *Urim* and *Thummim*, inscribed in Hebrew letters upon it, and the Latin words, *Lux et Veritas*, around it, signifying, probably, that light and truth are to be obtained by inquiring of the Lord. Brown University has a red cross on a white field between four open books, illuminated by a sun rising amid clouds, bearing the motto, *In Deo Speramus.* Dartmouth, established originally on the frontiers of our civilization, partly to educate converted natives, bears among other emblems the open book, the cross, a forest of Indians bending towards a college building, with the words, *Vox clamantis in deserto.* Our own college exhibits on its seal an open Bible with a full-orbed, unclouded sun pouring down upon its pages, and the words beneath it, *Terras irradient.* Such was the design of very pleasant and accommodate," but a stronghold of orthodoxy, it having been "kept spotless from the contagion of the opinions,"[1] i.e. "the

nearly all our American colleges, and such ought to be their mission. They set themselves up as the world's teachers: let them take care, lest, by moral unsoundness or neglect, they become the world's destroyers."

The words of Mr. Clifford were spoken at the inauguration of President Eliot:

"In the progress of what is complacently called the 'advanced thought of New England,' and it may be at no distant day, there doubtless will be waged a conflict of opinion of the highest import to the cause of truth and the welfare of the race.

"Whenever it comes, Harvard College can hold no subordinate place among the institutions of the country, in whose armories must be forged the weapons with which it will be fought. Her friends can have no misgivings as to the position she will occupy on such a field. Her great influence can never be arrayed on the side of those whose arrogant self-conceit can find no higher object of worship than the pretentious intellect of man — to-day, asserting its own omnipotence; to-morrow, 'babbling of green fields,' as its possessor sinks beneath the turf that covers them to mingle with his kindred clod; of those whose misty speculations shut out the life-giving rays of the 'Star of Bethlehem,' and who, with puny but presumptuous hand, would, —

——— "'hang a curtain on the East,
The daylight from the world to keep.'"

[1] Mather's Magnalia, III. 87.

Antinomian and Familisticall errors," and being favored with the "enlightened and powerful ministry" of Thomas Shepard.[1]

The clergy of course rallied around the College, giving it all their influence, which, at that period, was very great, and what they could of their substance, which was necessarily small. The people generally, if they had not enjoyed the advantages of a liberal education, had sat under an educated ministry, and were anxious to transmit the same privileges to their posterity. Hence we find them making their offerings to the infant College, some, of their abundance, the majority, of their poverty. In 1640, John Newgate of Boston made a donation of "five pounds per annum forever, towards the maintenance of lawfull, usefull, and good literature therein, and chiefly to the furtherance of the knowledge of Jesus Christ, and his word and will." Peirce, in his History of the College, speaks "of a number of sheep bequeathed by one man, a quantity of cotton cloth worth nine shillings presented by another, a pewter flagon worth ten shillings by a third, a fruit-dish, a sugar-spoon, a silver-tipt jug, one great salt, one

1 Thos. Shepard's Mem.

small trencher-salt, by others ; and of presents or legacies amounting severally to five shillings, nine shillings, one pound, two pounds &c.,"— showing the liberal views and spirit of the people, even when the colony was poor and struggling with the stern experiences of a settlement in the wilderness. "The earliest, the noblest, and the purest tribute to religion and science, this western world had yet witnessed," was, says Quincy, made in 1638, by John Harvard.

CHAPTER V.

ON his removal to Cambridge, Mr. Dunster united with Mr. Shepard's church, now the First Church of Cambridge, at which time he gave his Confession of faith and an account of the "Lord's personal dealings" with his soul. Except in one point, he was in full accord with the church, and that difference was not deemed a bar to fellowship. He held to the baptism of infants, but that immersion had the preponderance of proof in its favor. He told the church, however, that, as "there was something for sprinkling in the Scriptures, he should not be offended when [it] was used."[1]

In June of the next year (1641), he married Mrs. Elisabeth Glover,[2] the widow of Rev. Jesse

[1] See pages 109 and 260.

[2] This marriage resulted in a somewhat intimate connection between the Dunster and Winthrop families, by the subsequent

Glover,[1] who, in 1638, had died on his passage from England. There was no issue from this union, but he became the guardian of Mr. Glover's five children, a trust which he seems to have executed as "a kind and watchful parent, a faithful and considerate instructor."[2] Mrs. Dunster died in August, 1643, a little more than two years after their marriage, and sometime the next year, Mr. Dunster took a second wife, also named Elisabeth, a native of England, by whom he had five children, three sons and two daughters, all of whom were born in Cambridge. Mrs. Dunster survived her husband more than thirty years, dying at an advanced age in Cambridge.

Mr. Dunster became a freeman in 1641, a privilege then limited to church-members, and we

marriage of two of Mrs. Glover's daughters to sons of Governor Winthrop; and it was in this way, doubtless, that the latter's "Christian Experience," given in Hon. Robert C. Winthrop's "Life and Letters" (II. 165) of his illustrious ancestor, came into Mr. Dunster's possession. The copy from the lost original, in the "Dunster MS." in the Library of the Mass. Hist. Society, is in the President's clear and beautiful handwriting. "The neatness of his copy," says Mr. Winthrop, "attests the interest which he attached to it."

[1] See page 91. [2] MS. of Mr. Harris.

occasionally meet with his name in connection with various town and colonial affairs.

His pulpit services were very acceptable to the churches, for "as a preacher of the truths of Christ," he was, says Captain Johnston, "very powerful through his blessing to move the affections;" and after the death of Mr. Shepard, in 1649, he was called to "supply" the church at Cambridge until the election of a new pastor. In 1642, he was a member of a council of ministers and other delegates convened at Woburn to constitute a church in that town; and sometime afterwards assisted at the ordination of a pastor over the church.

Mr. Dunster took a deep interest in the conversion and education of the Indians. At the time of the settlement of New England, they probably numbered, within the Plymouth and Massachusetts colonies, between eight and nine thousand souls.[1] The Mayhews, father and son, and John Eliot felt themselves specially called to labor for the spiritual welfare of these savage tribes, and not without remarkable results. By the year 1674, within a period of thirty years,

[1] Palfrey. Hist. New England, III. 137.

there were about 4,000 "praying Indians" in New England, 1,100 of whom were connected with Mr. Eliot's congregations in Massachusetts.[1] In 1647, President Dunster,[2] with other ministers, "besides many other Christians," went out to Nonantum [Newton] to attend Mr. Eliot's Indian lecture, a scene of exceeding interest. Lechford, the Boston lawyer, had already, several years before, spoken of Mr. Dunster's zeal in this missionary work: "Master Henry Dunster, schoolmaster of Cambridge, deserves commendations above many; he hath the platform and way of conversion of the natives indifferent right, and much studies the same, wherein yet he wants not opposition, as some other also have met with: He will without doubt prove an instrument of much good in the country, being a good scholar, and having skill in the tongues. He will make it good that the way to instruct the Indians must be in their own language, not English, and that their language may be perfected."[3]

It was during his administration, that provision was made by the Commissioners of the Col-

[1] I. Mass. Hist. Col. I. [2] Clear Sunshine &c.

[3] Plain Dealing &c.

onies for the education, at Cambridge, of young men "to be helpful in teaching such Indian children as should be taken into the College for that end;" and in the second charter of the College, obtained in 1650, on his express petition, its object was declared to include "the education of the English and *Indian* youth of this country in knowledge and godliness." As the result in part, no doubt, of his zealous efforts in this direction, a brick building, called the Indian College, was erected, in 1665, within the college grounds.[1]

[1] Peirce. Hist. Harvard College, p. 28.

CHAPTER VI.

COTTON MATHER[1] thus describes the doings at Cambridge before Mr. Dunster's election to the Presidency: "While these things were a doing, a society of scholars to lodge in the new nests were forming under the conduct of one Mr. Nathaniel Eaton, a blade, who marvellously deceived the expectations of good men concerning him; for he was one fitter to be the master of a Bridewell than a Colledge; and though his avarice was notorious enough to get the name of Philargyrius fixed upon him, yet his cruelty was more scandalous than his avarice. He was a rare scholar himself, and he made many more such; but their education was truly in the school of Tyrannus. Among many other instances of his cruelty, he gave one in causing two men to hold a young gentleman, while he so unmercifully

[1] Magnalia, Bk. IV. p. 126.

beat him with a cudgel, that, upon complaint of it unto the Court, in 1639, he was fined an hundred marks, besides a convenient sum to be paid to the young gentleman that had suffered by his unmercifulness." Mr. Eaton and his wife seem to have been as well matched as Ananias and Sapphira, for while he was unmerciful in discipline, she was equally so in parsimony. While he flogged, she starved, the students, it being the custom for them to board in Commons.

The work before Mr. Dunster was of no ordinary character, demanding for its execution rare qualifications; not only learning, but administrative ability of a high order, a happy combination of suavity with firmness, and unbounded patience. In all respects he was found equal to the highest expectations that had been formed of him. "That which was before but at best *schola illustra*, grew to the stature and perfection of a College, and flourished in the profession of all liberal sciences."[1] Indeed it "soon acquired so high a reputation, that in several instances youth of opulent families in the parent country were sent over to receive their education in New Eng-

[1] Hubbard. Hist. of N. England.

land."[1] "As good instruction," says Peirce, "was offered here as at the first schools in the Old World."

The whole system of instruction and government, modelled, as far as circumstances would allow, after the plan of the English Universities, especially Cambridge, had now to be drawn up, and the means for putting it in operation, for the most part to be created, and mainly by the President's personal efforts. Besides the business of instruction and discipline, which largely devolved upon him, he had the supervision of the interests of the College in general and particular; including personal communication or correspondence with leading men in the four Colonies, appeals to the General Court and the Commissioners of the United Colonies, as well as the completion of the College edifice,[2] the erection of a President's

1 Palfrey. Hist. of N. England. Johnson's Wonder-Working Providence, and Mather's Magnalia.

2 "The edifice is very fair and comely within and without, having in it a spacious Hall (where they daily meet at Commons, Lectures, Exercises) and a large Library with some books in it, the gifts of diverse of our friends, their chambers and studies also fitted for, and possessed by the students, and all other rooms of office necessary and convenient."

house, the direction of Commons Hall, and finally the collection of his own salary. In fact, he was Treasurer as well as President. The President's house was built by funds derived from his friends by personal appeals or drawn from his own scanty means. The students' bills were generally paid, too, in various commodities,[1] which, however useful some of them might be in the family of the President or in Commons hall, must have been attended with no little inconvenience in meeting various liabilities of the College. Thus sheep, calves and cows, wheat, corn, apples and parsnips, butter, sugar and *malt*, beef and lamb, satin and cotton, are enumerated as among the College revenues.

The requisites of admission, introduced by Mr. Dunster, were "so much Latin as was sufficient to understand Tully, or any like classical author, and to make and speak true Latin, in prose and verse, and so much Greek as was included in declining perfectly the paradigms of the Greek nouns and verbs." The College

[1] From the scarcity of coin especially when immigration fell off, or from 1640, grain was made a legal tender for the payment of debts. Hildreth, I.

course[1] embraced the study of arithmetic, geometry, rhetoric, logic, ethics, physics, metaphysics, and divinity, and of Hebrew, Chaldee and Syriac.

[1] In the seventeenth century, in the English Cambridge, the purest Greek and Latin authors were not always studied. Patristic literature was much in vogue. Rhetoric and logic, pure and applied, were the leading studies — "the logic of Aristotle and the commentaries of the schoolmen." Aquinas, Daneus, &c. were in use. Mathematics were altogether subordinate to logic and metaphysics. Arithmetic, a little geography, and such astronomy as was then taught, were embraced in the College course. Theology was learned chiefly from private tutors, under whom also the Greek and Latin classics could be read more extensively than in the regular curriculum. "The crowning test of excellence consisted in the public disputations. . . . The most distinguished men in the University frequently engaged in them, and with an ardor which seems puerile when we recollect that the exhibition was really worthless in respect of the results attained, and simply represented a passage of arms between two accomplished masters of fence, wherein all the laws and by-laws of a rigorous logic were mercilessly enforced. . . . Haddon, in a letter to Dr. Cox, speaking of a public disputation, Sir Thomas Smith at a Cambridge Commencement, uses the following language: 'Had he [Dr. Cox] been there he would have heard another Solomon; that he caught the forward disputants as it were in a net with his questions; and that he concluded the most profound cases in philosophy with great gravity and deep knowledge.'" Mullinger. Cambridge Characteristics in the Seventeenth Century.

Twice a day, at prayers in the hall, the students read the Scriptures, "out of Hebrew into Greek, from the Old Testament in the morning, and out of English into Greek, from the New Testament, in the evening."[1] There were weekly declamations and public disputations. Latin was the only language allowed to be used on the College premises. From time to time the President was accustomed "to preach on Lord's day in Cambridge," for the special benefit of the students, who had "a particular gallery allotted unto them," and they were required to "commonplace" these and other sermons, and repeat them in the College hall.

Among the "Rules and Precepts" of the Dunster code were the following, which were published in Latin :

"Let every student be plainly instructed, and earnestly pressed to consider well, the maine end of his life and studies is, *to know God and Jesus Christ, which is eternall life*, and therefore to lay Christ at the bottome, as the only foundation of all sound knowledge and learning."

"They shall honor, as their parents, the ma

[1] Magnalia, B. IV. and N. England's First Fruits.

gistrates, elders, tutors, and *all who are older than themselves*, as reason requires, being silent in their presence, except when asked a question, not contradicting, but showing all those marks of honor and reverence which are in praiseworthy use, saluting them with a bow, standing uncovered &c."

"Let them be slow to speak. Let them avoid not only oaths, lies, and scandal, but also nonsense, scurrility, levity, ribaldry, and all offensive carriages."

"Let no one be a busy-body."

"Every undergraduate, unless he be a fellow-commoner (commensalis), the son of a gentleman, or man of superior rank (nobilis), or the eldest son of a knight (miles), shall be called by his surname only."

"No student shall buy, sell or exchange any thing of the value of sixpence, without the approbation of his parent, guardian or tutor."

"The scholars shall under no pretext use the vernacular tongue, unless a public English exercise has been assigned them."

"If any student shall violate the law of God or

of this College, either from perverseness or from gross negligence, after he shall have been twice admonished, he may *be whipped* (virgis coerceatur), if not an adult [eighteen]; but if an adult, his case shall be laid before the overseers, that notice may be publicly taken of him according to his deserts.[1] In case of graver offences, however, let no one expect such gradual proceedings, or that an admonition must necessarily be repeated in relation to the same law." [2]

Quincy [3] says that "the principles of education established under the authority of Mr. Dunster" were not "materially changed during the whole of the seventeenth century."

The above system of instruction and discipline

1 Sometimes unruly College boys were turned over to the civil authorities, as the following extract from the records of the Middlesex County Court, held in Cambridge, June 9, 1656, will show: "Thomas Parish, a student of Harvard College, being convicted before this Court of some foolish and inordinate carriages toward the Towne and Church of Cambridge, at a public meeting, was admonished by the Court, and enjoined to make acknowledgments of his fault therein at their next public meeting, &c."

2 See New England's First Fruits, and Mass. Hist. Coll. I. 242.

3 History of Harvard College, I. 191.

was borrowed in part from the English universities,[1] and in some respects strikingly displays

[1] At the period when Mr. Dunster was pursuing his University course, the government consisted of a Chancellor, Vice-chancellor, High Steward, Proctors, Taxors, the Esquire Bedells [beadles], &c.; and its courts held almost exclusive jurisdiction over those who resided within its corporate limits. The University had its own police, who were supposed to act in concert with the town constables. The Proctors, who were resident graduates, clergymen, and unmarried, were guardians of the public morals for the special protection of the students, having power to search the town, and even to enter houses, for persons "suspected of evil," particularly suspected females, and to have them arraigned before the University tribunals.

The authority of the University also extended further, the Vice-chancellor having the exclusive right of granting licenses for the sale of wine in the town of Cambridge, for ale-houses in Cambridge and the adjacent village of Chesterton, and for theatrical performances within fourteen miles of the town. The supervision of weights and measures within the town and suburbs, and of the markets and Fairs, and the inspection of provisions, belonged to the University. The Taxors, who were resident graduates, Masters of Arts, and generally also clergymen, were intrusted with this special duty, relieving the monotony of literary labor by looking after weights, measures, markets, and meats. The Esquire Bedells were chiefly ornamental, holding up the dignity of the University and its high officials by attending the Chancellor &c. with their staves on public occasions, besides sundry other useless performances. Most of these rules and customs are now in vogue in the English universities, the spirit of the times. For a hundred and thirty years, that is, down to 1773, the names of students at Harvard were arranged upon the catalogue, not in alphabetical order, but according to the social standing.[1]

"The application of both official and conventional titles was [at that time] a matter of careful observance. Only a small number of persons of the best condition had the designation Mr. or Mrs. prefixed to their names. . . . Goodman and Goodwife were the appropriate addresses of persons above the condition of servitude and below that

though efforts have been made in Parliament for abolishing some of them. Cambridge University Commission, Vol. 44.

The discipline of a German University is conducted by a University magistrate, in conjunction with the Rector, the Senate, and the Dean of the Faculties. The modes of correction are personal remonstrance, solitary confinement in the University lock-up, of three days for minor, and not more than a month for graver offences, and lastly expulsion. Thomson. Almae Matres.

The experience of American Colleges favors an important modification of the academic government of students. There is no good reason why college criminals should fare better or otherwise than similar offenders outside Parnassus. The law of the land should show no favoritism.

[1] See Cong. Quart. XIII. 257.

of gentility."[1] In church, the congregation was carefully seated in accordance with this aristocratic principle; and, when a new meetinghouse was opened for worship, one of the most important duties was the appointment of a committee to attend to this delicate service.

The practice of corporal punishment early and long flourished in the English universities. It is alluded to amusingly in Sir John Fenn's Collection of Letters of the Paston Family, in the time of Henry VI. and by Dr. Johnson in a characteristic manner, in his Life of Milton: "I am ashamed to relate, what I *fear* is true, that Milton was the last student, in either University, that suffered the public indignity of corporal

[1] Palfrey, II. 67. Winthrop's Journal has the following record: — "1631, Aug. 27. At a court, one Josias Plaistowe and two of his servants were censured for stealing corn &c. . . . the master to restore twofold, and to be degraded from the title of a gentleman."

In a note appended to the History of The Old South Church, it is stated, that "the title of Mr. was given to those who had taken a second degree in College [*Sir* was the title of bachelors of arts], to all magistrates, to all who were or had been military officers as high as captain, to those on whose coats-of-arms was inscribed 'generosus,' to merchants of standing, and perhaps to some others."

punishment." "In Trinity College [Cambridge], there was a regular service [of this kind] in the Hall every Thursday evening at seven o'clock, in the presence of all the undergraduates, on such junior delinquents as had been reserved for the ceremony during the week."[1] At the New England Cambridge, "the tutors chastised at discretion, and on very solemn occasions the overseers were called together, either to authorize or witness the execution of the severer punishments."[2] Judge Sewall, in his Diary,[3] relates an instance, which occurred in 1674, during the presidency of Mr. Hoar. On the charge of "speaking blasphemous words," the offender, after an examination by the government, was transferred to the Corporation, who, after advising with the Overseers, sentenced him to be "publickly whipped before all the scholars," to be "suspended as to taking his degree of Bachelor," to "sit alone by himself in the Hall uncovered at meals, during the pleasure of the President and Fellows,"[4] to be "obedient in all

[1] Masson. Life and Times of Milton.

[2] Quincy. [3] See Peirce.

[4] "For more than fifty years after the foundation of the Col-

things, doing what exercise was appointed him by the President, or else be finally expelled the College." The sentence was twice read before him in the presence of the President and Fellows, the Committee, and the scholars, when he kneeled down, and the President having offered prayer, "Goodman[1] Hely," the prison-keeper[2] at Cambridge, on a sign from the President, "*attended . . . to the performance of his part in the work.*" The solemn exercise was closed by prayer from the President.

It would seem that the ingenuous youths at

lege, the tutors, who assisted the President in instruction and government, were called 'Fellows of the College.'" Peirce. They were resident graduates.

[1] Page 69.

[2] Thirty years before, the President personally "attended to the performance" of this part of the work, as we learn from Winthrop's Journal (2: 166).—"May, 4, 1644. Two of our ministers' sons, being students in the College, robbed two dwelling houses in the night, of some 15 pounds. Being found out, they were ordered by the governours of the College to be there whipped, which was performed by the president himself—yet they were about 20 years of age; and after they were brought into the Court and ordered to twofold satisfaction, or to serve so long for it. We had yet no particular punishment for burglary."

Harvard, or their tender-hearted parents, must have rebelled against the College rod, for in 1645, in a Petition to the "Much Honored the Commissioners of the United Colonies," President Dunster, "for his more free, conscionable, prudent and unblameable administration of his place," desired their consideration of the following, among other queries:

"1. Whether you be willing to submit the youth of your Colonies that be or shall be students so far to the College discipline administered by the President and Fellows, and in cases arduous by the advice of the Overseers, that *whatsoever punishments* shall be inflicted for their demerits according to the laws of said College, shall no ways infringe any privileges or honorable exhibition[1] from your Colonies to the College, and whether you do not give your approbation to said laws?"[2] And in 1654, the General Court of Massachusetts was induced to give its sanction to the flogging system, as follows: "It is ordered by this Court that the president and

[1] A term derived from the English Universities for an allowance or bounty for the maintenance of scholars.

[2] Mass. State Archives. Vol 58, p. 9.

fellows of Harvard College for the time being, or the major part of them, are hereby empowered according to their best discretion, to punish all misdemeanors of the youth in their society, either by fine, or *whipping* in the hall, openly, as the nature of the offence shall require, not exceeding ten shillings or ten stripes for one offence."[1]

Even as late as 1734, nearly a hundred years after the foundation of the College, the revised body of Laws provides for the bodily chastisement of students: "It shall be lawful for the President, Tutors, and Professors, to punish undergraduates by *Boxing*, when they shall judge the nature or circumstance of the offence call for it." And in 1746, it could only be said that "corporal punishment was *going out* of use."[2]

While upon the subject of College discipline, we must not omit to mention a tradition about Mr. Dunster, "still extant among his descendants, that one day being at Concord, he suddenly ordered his horse to be saddled, as he must immediately return to Cambridge. On be-

[1] Mass. Col. Records III. 417.

[2] Peirce, page 228.

ing asked the cause of his abrupt departure, he replied, that he had received word that the students there had raised the Evil One, — a practice, if we may believe the stories of recent College boys, not yet obsolete, though understood by them in a very different light from what it was in former times — and being unable to control his Satanic Majesty's exhibitions, had become alarmed.

On arriving at Cambridge, he took his well-filled powder-horn, and pouring a part of its contents on the floor, abjured the presence of the ugly visitor, and, to the relief of the affrighted boys, directly flashed him out of the College. It is added, that Satan, when thus summarily sent away, was heard to say, that he would never trouble the Dunsters afterwards,[1] a consoling assurance, which helps us to fix the date of this terrific appearance. It must have been posterior to Mr. Mitchell's remarkable interview with Mr. Dunster, upon the subject of infant baptism, when he ascertained, to his horror, that the hith-

[1] We have quoted from a speech delivered at the Mason (N.H.) centennial celebration, by Samuel Dunster Esq., of Attleboro,' Mass., a descendant of President Dunster.

erto considered pious President, was then troubled, if not inspired, by the "Evil One."[1]

If the tradition is more than a myth, — and it has come down in two distinct lines of the Dunster family, — it would seem probable, that the students, according to the peculiar belief of that age in the active agency of Satan in human affairs, were really persuaded that he was showing himself off among them in certain terrible ways, and that the President dispelled the illusion by a shrewd but harmless artifice, which, we may readily imagine, he secretly enjoyed at the expense of his credulous and timorous juniors.

[1] See page 106.

CHAPTER VII.

BESIDES the proper duties which pertained to his office, it belonged to Mr. Dunster, in those days of straitened means and primitive simplicity, to prepare rules for the regulation of the steward's department, and to give personal attention to its management. He was expected to issue disbursements to the steward, butler or cook, for the maintenance of the commons, and to receive a quarterly report of the same, including an inventory of all the College utensils and vessels, great and small, and their condition at the time. It appears that while the butler and cook were "to see that the said utensils were kept clean and sweet," they were "not bound to keep or cleanse any particular scholar's spoons, cup, or such like, but at their own discretion." These same officials were also "to see that all the rooms peculiar to their offices, together with their appurtenances, be daily set and kept in order, clean and sweet from all manner of noisomeness and nastiness or sensible offensiveness." And "whereas much inconvenience falleth out of the scholars' bringing candles in course into the Hall, therefore the butler shall receive henceforth at the President's or Steward's hands twenty shillings towards candles for the Hall, for prayer-time and supper, which, that it may not be burdensome, it shall be put proportionably upon every scholar who retaineth his seat in the buttery."

By no express law, but according to English traditions, "Freshmen were a kind of servitors to the whole College out of studying hours, to go of errands," and perform various menial services, — a custom, which, in later times, has been superseded by "hazing," a practice more annoying, it may be, but less degrading, except to those who practise it.

The Library was of course small during Mr. Dunster's Presidency, consisting chiefly of 320 volumes contributed by John Harvard, in 1638, and of books given by magistrates from their libraries, in 1642, to the value of two hundred pounds. Further donations were doubtless made by ministers and others. A note given by Mr. Dunster, preserved on the College records, "is a curious evidence," says Quincy, "of the scarcity of books at that period, and of the value attached to them:" —

"These presents witness, that whereas Joshua Scottow,[1] of Boston, merchant, hath of his own free accord procured for the library of Harvard College, Henry Stephens his Thesaurus, in four volumes, in folio, and bestowed the same thereon, it is on this condition, and with this promise following; that if ever the said Joshua, during his life, shall have occasion to use the said book, or any parcel thereof, he shall have free liberty thereof, and access thereto. And if God shall bless the said Joshua with any child, or children, that shall be students of the Greek tongue, then the said books above specified shall be unto them delivered, in case that they will not otherwise be satisfied without it.

[1] Mr. Scottow "seems to have been the earliest person in the Colony who had an antiquarian turn of mind." In 1691 he wrote "Old Men's Fears for their own Declensions; mixed with fears of their and posterity's further falling off New England's primitive constitution." Young's Chron. of Mass.

"In witness whereof this present writing is signed by me, Henry Dunster, President of the College, aforesaid, made at Boston, this twenty-eighth day of the eighth month, 1649.

HENRY DUNSTER."

In his letter to the Commissioners,[1] in 1645, Mr. Dunster, in fitting and forcible words, called their attention to the state of the Library: "Seeing the public library in the College is yet defective in all manner of books, specially in law, physics, philosophy, and mathematics, the furnishing whereof would be both honorable and profitable to the country in general and in special to the scholars, whose various inclinations to all professions might thereby be encouraged and furthered; we therefore humbly entreat to use such means as your wisdom shall think meet for supply of the same."[2]

The subject of "fellowships" is awakening very considerable interest among the friends of learn-

[1] See page 34. State Archives, vol. 58, p. 9.

[2] In 1764 the Library contained 5,000 volumes. That year it was consumed by fire. It now numbers 150,000 volumes. Within a radius of six or seven miles of Boston, there are nearly 800,000 volumes in public libraries.

ing at the present time, and has been ably discussed in a paper read before an Educational Convention,[1] by one of our ripest scholars.[2] It has long been a part of the College system of England, at Oxford and Cambridge, and in a modified form, ought to be introduced into our American colleges. It contemplates the provision, by a special fund, for a post-graduate course of study by eminent scholars, far beyond the usual limits of the College curriculum, so that from this body of learned men "may go forth, year by year, accomplished teachers, preachers, and writers, to positions of the highest influence."

Such a plan, even in the infancy of the College and poverty of the Colony, was inaugurated by President Dunster at Cambridge, and commended by him to the liberality of the people, through the Commissioners of the United Colonies, — a proof of his broad and generous views of education. He wrote: "Whereas it is expedient that pious, diligent, and learned graduates

[1] Proceedings of The National Baptist Educational Convention, 1870.

[2] Rev. Dr. Hovey, President of the Newton Theological Institution, and Professor of Theology.

should be elected fellows as emergent occasions shall require, and that then they should have for their encouragement the stipend due from such scholars as are under their tuition, which for the present is a considerable part of the President's maintenance ; therefore, we humbly entreat you to state what you think to be a meet allowance for the President, and whence it shall arise."

Prof. Hovey recommends that $10,000 be the basis of a fellowship, yielding an income of $600 or $700. President Dunster suggested to the Commissioners "£16 per annum for a fellowship."

The scantiness and irregularity of his own salary[1] — at one period unpaid for two years — did not prevent his appeals on behalf of deserving "scholars,"[2] for whom, as well as for "fellows," he

1 "Dunster was a man of marked excellence of character; learned, religious, conscientious, charitable and forgiving. He labored and suffered for the good of the College, and expended of his substance in its service. His insufficient and meagre salary was paid, not in cash, but by transfers of town-rates, of which he was enforced to be the collector, suffering all the attending delays, vexations, depreciations, and losses." Willard Memoir, p. 179, n.

2 ". . . And besides, he [Mr. Dunster] having a good in-

urged the General Court and the Colonial Commissioners to make provision. Two years before this (1643), writing to Governor Winthrop,[1] he had said: "I have suffered abatements from[2] £60 to £50, from £50 to £45, from £45 to £30, which is now my rent from the [Charlestown] ferry."[3] But he added with characteristic nobleness: "I was and am willing, considering the poverty of the country, to descend to the lowest

spection into the well-ordering of things for the students' maintenance (whose commons hath been very short hitherto) by his frugal providence hath continued them longer at their studies than otherwise they could have done; and verily it's great pity such ripe heads as many of them be, should want means to further them in learning." Wonder-Working Providence.

[1] Mass. Hist. Collec. II. Ser. X. 187.

[2] The salaries of ministers at that time ranged from £30 to £90. Mr. Symmes of Charlestown had the largest, Mr. Cotton and three others had £80, five others £70, six others £60, and so on, the pastor at Reading having the smallest, £30. Felt's Eccles. Hist. Poole's Introd. to Wonder-Working Prov.

[3] In 1650, the General Court passed the following order:

"The President is authorised to dispose of the Charles Towne ferry, by lease or otherwise, making the best and most advantage thereof to his own content, so as those to whom he dispose it unto perform the service, and keep sufficient boats for the use thereof, as the order of Court requires." Col. Records, III. 214.

step, if there can be nothing comfortably allowed me ; I will sit down appeased desiring no more but what may supply me and mine with food and raiment (and to give every one their own), to the furtherance of the success of our labors for the good of Church and Commonwealth, without distraction in the work whereunto I am called, and by God's great mercy and goodness cheerfully therein abide ; desiring your prayers for a continuance, and your praises to God for the sanctifying of all the passages of his fatherly providence towards

Your loving and much bounden servant,

HENRY DUNSTER."

In this spirit of Christian self-denial, he more than met the requirement of the Roman poet :

> Rebus augustis animosus atque
> Fortis appare.

Two years after Mr. Dunster went to Cambridge, a class of nine young men "of good hope" was found prepared for graduation, and accordingly the first Commencement took place in 1642, only fourteen years after the settlement at Salem, and twenty-two after the arrival of the Mayflower. This gathering of the first-fruits of his labors in the College must have been an occasion of special interest to the President, as well as highly gratifying to the colonists generally. Here, on the borders of a yet unbroken wilderness, almost within sight of Indian wigwams, were assembled the dignitaries of the Colony, the learned ministers of the neighborhood, and others, to reproduce in humbler style the scholastic ceremonies in which so many of them, with "pomp and circumstance," had participated, in the Universities of old England. Governor Hutchinson[1] has preserved the record of the occasion, from which we learn that "the chief exercises were disputations[2] on theses or questions in Logic, Ethics, Natural Philosophy and most of the liberal arts, which the defendant had published beforehand on a sheet of paper, and obliged himself to answer all objections brought against them."[3] Some of these theses are curious, as showing the state of learning, and the subjects and habits of thought, at that period, not only in New England but in Europe. They were in

[1] Hist. I, 510. [2] Page 64, note.

[3] Neal's History of New England.

Latin, and were discussed in the same language. We fear that some of our modern candidates for the Bachelor's degree, not to say of the Master's, would find even the translation of some of these theses[1] a hazardous experiment.

Of the graduates of 1642, two became quite eminent, — George Downing (the nephew of Hugh Peter), who attained high distinction under Cromwell, and was knighted by Charles II., and William Hubbard, as historian of New England.

Besides the management of the College, Mr. Dunster maintained a correspondence with literary and Christian friends abroad. A letter to Ravius,[2] a distinguished Oriental scholar, then

[1] Pages 268–270.

[2] "Ravius or Ravis was a native of Berlin, born in 1613, and, in order to advance himself in the knowledge of the Oriental languages, travelled in the East, where he learned Turkish, Persian and Arabic, bringing back some precious manuscripts. At Utrecht, Kiel, and Frankfort-on-the-Main, as well as in London, he taught the languages generally termed Oriental, and published several works on his favorite subject. By letters from Dr. Elichman, De Dieu and Vossius, he was introduced to Archbishop Usher, who patronized him liberally, and to whom he dedicated his 'General Grammar for the ready attaining the Ebrew, Sa-

residing in London, who was deeply interested in the progress of learning and religion in America, has been preserved, and is proof of the writer's philological tastes and foreign reputation. It acknowledges favors to the College in the donation of valuable books &c., but is mainly a reply to various questions proposed in a previous letter by his learned friend, relating to linguistic subjects, especially the Indian language, and the state of education and religion in the Colonies. In it he says:

"Yours of the 27th of February came to our hands, together with the box and all things therein mentioned, about the 2d or 3d of August, for which I am not only bounden to give thanks unto God for raising up such instruments to promote his kingdom not only in the places where they live, but also throughout all the world, to the utmost of their power. But I am also further desired, from my occasions in the College, to

maritan, Calde, Syriac, Arabic, and the Ethiopic languages.' Grotius introduced him to Cardinal Richelieu, and he visited the court of Christina of Sweden. He died at Frankfort, June 21, 1677." Note to IV. Hist. Col. I. 251. See also Chalmers. The entire letter is given in the Appendix.

return thanks unto yourself for your special good will, as to the whole country here in general, so in special to the promoting of learning in the College amongst the students, and in the woods amongst the Indians in their savage booths or wigwams. And albeit it extendeth only to the power to acknowledge such kindness without further external requitals, yet undoubtedly the Lord Jesus takes notice of all his faithful subjects' prayers and endeavors to enlarge his kingdom, and will here requite it with the perfume of a good name better than precious ointment, and hereafter with a Come, ye blessed of my Father, inherit the kingdom."

After a reference to the mission among the Indians, the letter concludes as follows:

"Lastly, we profess ourselves unable to answer the tender of your good will and propensity of spirit towards us, our infant College compared with the Academies in Europe being like Mantua unto Rome, and as unworthy to confine a man of your parts and place, as that small town the prince of the Latin poets. Yet, nevertheless, if divine providence should waft you over the Atlantic ocean, or if your spirit desire to see what sons of Seth wander in these woods, then Harvard College would think itself honored in your visit.

"Meantime, while God's providence continueth you where you be, as you tender your readiness to further our studies in the Oriental tongues, and have already given a real testimony of your benevolent and beneficent spirit, so, if God's providence put an opportunity into your hand that you help us with books of those languages from some able hands and willing hearts (for from yourself it were unreasonable to expect any more than such books as yourself are personally the author of) then should we be very glad and evermore thankful to you and them who shall procure us Buxtorf's Concordances and Bible (for the King of Spain's we have, and the King of France's Bible is more than we dare hope for) and whatsoever Hebrew, Chaldee, Syriac or Arabic authors, God's providence shall enlarge their hands and hearts to procure us. A wonderful impulse unto these studies lies on the spirits of our students, some of whom can with ease dextrously translate Hebrew and Chaldee into Greek.

"But I forget myself in detaining you so long

from your serious and more profitable studies. Let me hear, I pray, if you receive this my letter. The Lord be with you, and prosper all your endeavors. So, I entreat, pray for yours in the Lord."

CHAPTER VIII.

AS Massachusetts established the first College in North America, so also the first printing-press. It was in January, 1639, that the press procured in England by Rev. Jesse Glover, was set up in Cambridge, by direction of the magistrates and elders, as "an appendage of Harvard College."[1] It was considered to be too powerful an instrument for good or evil, to be

[1] Thomas. History of Printing.

No printing was allowed within the jurisdiction of Massachusetts, except at Cambridge. It was not till 1664, that permission was obtained to set up a press in Boston.

The printing for New Hampshire was done in Boston till 1756, in which year a press was established in Portsmouth.

The first Anglo-American newspaper — *The Boston News-Letter*, a weekly half-sheet — was printed April, 1704.

The first press in Virginia was set up in 1727. But Trübner (see Palfrey, II.: 45, n.) states, that there was no printing-press in the city of Exeter, England, till 1669, and none in Liverpool till 1749.

left in private hands, and accordingly from the first and for more than a hundred years[1] it was under the control of the General Court, though it was not till 1665[2] that licensers of the press were appointed by that body. But a sharp lookout was always had upon its issues, lest something deemed heretical or hurtful to the govern-

[1] "For preventing irregularities and abuse to the Authority of this Country by the printing Press, it is ordered by this Court and the Authority thereof that there shall be noe Printing press allowed in any towne within this jurisdiction but in Cambridge, nor shall any Person or Persons presume to print any Copie but by the allowance first had and obtayned, under the hands of such as this Court shall from time to time Impowre, the President of the Colledge, Mr. John Shearman, Mr. Jonathan Mitchell, and Mr. Thomas Shepard or any two of them, to survey such copie or copies, and to prohibit or allowe the same according to this order, and in case of non-Observance of this Order to forfeite the Press to the Country, and bee dissinabled from using any such profession within this Jurisdiction for the time to come, provided this Order shall not Extend to the Obstruction of any copie which this Court shall judge meet to Order to bee published in Print." State Archives, Vol., 58, 55.

[2] In 1667 the General Court suppressed the *Imitation of Christ*, by Thomas à Kempis, and that too, after the licensers had permitted its publication.

Legal restraints were not removed till 1755. Thomas. I. 246.

ment should by means of it find its way among the people.

On Mr. Dunster's marriage, in 1641, to the widow of Mr. Glover, the press, (which had come into her possession upon her husband's decease) was placed under his management, and its profits, in part at least, seem to have accrued to the revenues of the College. It was set up in the President's house, where it remained till 1655,[1] and he was appointed to supervise its publications. Its first contributions to American literature were the *Freeman's Oath,* Peirce's *Almanack,* and the *Psalms newly turned into Metre,* the last printed in 1640. Its issues were chiefly of a religious character; the most important being the works prepared by John Eliot in the Indian language, only one of which, however, the *Indian Catechism,* 1653, was printed while Mr. Dunster was its manager. "The press of Harvard Col-

[1] In the "Information given by the Corporation and Overseers to the General Court, 9 May, 1655," it is said: "The revenue of the press (which is but small) must at present be improved for the finishing of the print-house, its continuance in the President's house being (besides other inconveniences) dangerous and hurtful to the edifice itself."

lege was for a time as celebrated as the presses of the Universities of Oxford and Cambridge, in England."[1]

Mr. Dunster had a special connection with one work which issued from his press, a Psalm-Book. Previous to 1640, the version of Sternhold and Hopkins had been in use in most of the New England churches,[2] but as this work was not considered a sufficiently accurate rendering of the original, and its versification was too rugged for even our not very fastidious fathers, it was resolved to attempt a new translation of the Psalms of David. Three well known ministers, Richard Mather of Dorchester, and Eliot and Weld of Roxbury undertook the difficult task. In 1640, the result of their painful labors was given to an expectant public, from Mr. Dunster's house, under the title of, *The whole Booke of Psalmes Faithfully Translated into English Metre. Whereunto is prefixed a discourse declaring not only the lawfulness, but also the necessity of*

[1] Thomas.

[2] "The Plymouth Churches sang from the Psalter of Ainsworth through their whole history." Brigham, The Colony of New Plymouth.

the heavenly Ordinance of Singing Scripture Psalms in the churches of God.[1]

It is due to the authors to say, that they seem to have been modestly aware of the poetical defects of their work. "If," said they, in the Preface, "the verses are not always so smooth and elegant as some may desire or expect, let them consider that God's Altar needs not our polishings, Ex. 20: for wee have respected rather a plaine translation than to smooth our verses with the sweetness of any paraphrase, and soe have attended Conscience rather than Elegance, fidelity rather than poetry, in translating the Hebrew words into English language, and David's poetry into English meetre; that soe wee may sing in Sion the Lord's songs of prayse according to his own will; until hee take us from hence, and wipe away all our teares, and bid us enter into our master's joye to sing eternall Halleluiahs." This edition contained no hymns, but only psalms, all else being regarded quite in the light of a profanation of worship. But in the second

[1] Two copies of the first edition are in the Public Library of Boston, which also has an elegant reprint, edited by Dr. N. B. Shurtleff, with an Introduction.

edition (1647), the authors ventured to insert a few spiritual songs.

"It did not," however, says Neal, "satisfy the expectations of judicious men." "It was thought," says Cotton Mather, "that a little more of art was to be employed." Mr. Shepard of Cambridge was so much exercised about its metrical defects, that he despatched the following admonitory stanzas to the reverend authors, which can only make us wonder that such a master of verse should not have been intrusted with furnishing the psalmody of that generation:

"You Roxb'ry poets, keep clear of the crime
Of missing to give us very good rhyme.
And you of Dorchester, your verses lengthen,
But with the text's own words, you will them strengthen."[1]

The following specimen of the Psalm-Book of 1640 and 1647 will, we are sure, justify the criticism of Mr. Shepard and the general desire for an improved version:

PSALME I.

1 O Blessed man, that in th' advice
of wicked doth not walk:
Nor stand in sinners way, nor sit
in chayre of scornfull folk.

[1] Mather's Magnalia.

2 But in the law of Jehovah
  is his longing delight:
And in his law doth meditate,
  by day and eke by night.

"For a further improvement of the work," says Prince,[1] "it was committed to the Rev. Mr. Henry Dunstar, President of Harvard College, one of the greatest masters of the oriental languages, that hath been known in these ends of the earth." Associated with him in the task of *revising* and *polishing*, was Mr. Richard Lyon, tutor to Sir Henry Mildmay's son, then boarding in Mr. Dunster's house.

Nothing can be more certain than that neither of these excellent persons was blessed with poetic genius. The oriental learning necessary for the work of revision was probably supplied in the main by the President, and this, we judge, was worked up into something like poetry by the junior partner in the enterprise; for Mr. Lyon, we are told, added to the original work a large number of songs and hymns of his own composition. It is due to Mr. Dunster's memory to

[1] Preface to Revised Psalm-book, 1758.

relieve him, if possible, of the charge of furnishing the poetry.

Yet a real advance was made upon the production of the reverend bards of Dorchester and Roxbury, though considerably later, Neal, the historian of New England, suggested that the improved psalm-book needed "to be revised and corrected by the more *beautiful* verses of Dr. Patrick, Tate and Brady."

But, for that day, the New England Psalm-Book was a great achievement, and it was abundantly appreciated. First printed in 1650, it speedily came into use in the New England Churches, and obtained a large circulation in England and Scotland, passing through more than fifty editions at home and abroad. In England it was used in some churches as late as 1717, and in Scotland till 1750.

In sacred lyrics, as in material things, the world has made wonderful progress since Dunster's day; and it ill becomes us to severely criticise the ruder rhymes which aided the devotions of our fathers. Poor as they are now seen to be, they raised the thoughts of godly men and women in adoration and thanksgiving to the great

Supreme, and also helped to introduce our richer modern psalmody, to which so many gifted sons of song have contributed the choicest productions of their genius.

From the following specimen of the Dunster Psalm-Book, the 17th edition, our readers can form their own opinion of its poetic merit:

1 O Blessed man that walks not in
th' advice of wicked men,
Nor standeth in the sinners way,
nor scorners seat sits in.

2 But he upon Jehovah's law
doth set his whole delight,
And in his law doth meditate
both in the day and night.

3 He shall be like a planted tree
by water brooks which shall
In his due season yield his fruit,
whose leaf shall never fail:

4 And all he doth shall prosper well:
the wicked are not so:
But they are like unto the chaff
which wind drives to and fro.

5 Therefore shall not ungodly men
in judgment stand upright:
Nor in th' assembly of the just
shall stand the sinful wight.

6 For of the righteous men, the Lord
acknowledgeth the way:
Whereas the way of wicked men
shall utterly decay.[1]

[1] "For eighty or ninety years, it is said, not more than ten different tunes, if so many, were used in public worship. Few congregations could sing more than the five tunes now known by the names of York, Hackney, Windsor, St. Mary's and Martyrs. Instrumental music was proscribed." Palfrey, II. 41, note.

CHAPTER IX.

MR. DUNSTER had been President of the College for a period of twelve or thirteen years, when his public avowal of sentiments obnoxious to the dominant party in the Colony awakened an intense excitement against him,[1] resulting ultimately in his removal from office, and his exile to the more tolerant sister colony of Plymouth.

The narrative of events connected with his "martyrdom"[2] exhibits in a striking light the

1 "The orthodox spirit of the whole colony was instantly roused; and the strongest, because involuntary, testimony is borne to the intellectual power and moral influence of Dunster, by the alarm his defection excited, and the harsh measures dictated by that feeling; while his conscientiousness is attested by the meekness of his submission to the rebukes which were sternly administered." S. A. Eliot. Sketch of the History of Harvard College, 1848.

2 Quincy.

peculiar spirit of those times, and the nobleness of his own character. His independence of thought, his thorough conscientiousness, his firm adherence to what he believed to be God's truth, his readiness to sacrifice the dearest friendships and a position of high honor and wide influence, which also involved his most cherished plans of usefulness, all at the call of duty, and last and highest, his pious resignation to God's will, and his gentle and forgiving temper in the midst of great provocations, — these present him before us as one of the greatest and best men of his day. The lessons of those events can never be obsolete.

Neal, an early historian of New England, thus gives in brief the reasons of Mr. Dunster's removal: "The Overseers were uneasy because he had declared himself an Anabaptist, fearing lest he should instil those principles into the youth that were under his care." One of the Puritan fathers of Massachusetts, whose father was a President of the College, and who would have liked to have been one himself, Cotton Mather, shall state the case as he understood it: "Among those of our fathers, who differed somewhat from his brethren, was that learned and worthy man, Mr. Henry Dunster. . . . Wonderfully falling into the errors of Antipaedobaptism, the overseers of the College became solicitous that the students there might not be unawares ensnared in the errors of the President. Wherefore they labored with an extreme agony either to rescue the good man from his own mistake, or to restrain him from imposing them upon the hope of the flock, of both which, finding themselves to despair, they did, as quietly as they could, procure his removal, and provide him a successor in Mr. Charles Chauncy."[1] In another place[2] he says more fully: "Our Mitchel,[3] presently upon his becoming pastor of Cambridge, met with a more than

[1] Magnalia. Book III. 367. [2] Book IV. 78.

[3] Rev. Jonathan Mitchell, who succeeded Thomas Shepard as pastor at Cambridge, was born in England in 1624, and was graduated at Harvard College, where he was called the "glory of the College," in 1649. He had an extraordinary reputation, even while a young man, for piety and accomplishments, and was styled the "matchless" Mitchell. As a preacher, he managed his subjects with an "extraordinary invention, curious disposition, and copious application." "He would speak with such a transcendent majesty and liveliness, that the people would often shake under his dispensations, as if they heard the sound of the trumpets from the burning mountains." His wonderful success

ordinary trial, in that the good man who was then President of the Colledge, and a member of the Church there, was unaccountably fallen into the briars of Antipaedobaptism ; and being briar'd in the scruples of that persuasion, he not only forbore to present an infant of his own unto the Baptism of our Lord, but also thought himself under some obligation to bear his testimony in some sermons against the administration of baptism to any infant whatsoever. The brethren of the church were somewhat vehement and violent in their signifying of their dissatisfaction at the obstruction, which the renitencies of that gentleman threatened with the peaceable practice of infant-baptism, wherein they had hitherto walked; and judged it necessary for the vindication of the

in dealing with errorists is set forth in the following stanzas from an Elegy by a young friend of his :

> "The Quaker trembling at his thunder fled,
> And with Caligula resum'd his bed.
> The Munster goblin, by his holy flood
> Exorcis'd, like a thin phantasma stood."

Strange that a man who could so shake his audiences, and deal so vigorously with heretics, should have been so marvellously shaken by the "Munster goblin," in the shape of Mr. Dunster. See Magnalia, II. 79, 80.

Church's name abroad in the country, and for the safety of the Congregation at home, to desire of him that he would cease preaching as formerly, until he had better satisfied himself in the point now doubted by him. At these things extream was the uneasiness of our Mitchel, who told the brethren that more light and less heat would do better; but yet saw the zeal of some against this good man's error, to push the matter on so far, that being but a young man, he was likely now to be embarrassed in a controversy with so considerable a person, and with one who had been his tutor, and a worthy and godly man. He could give this account of it: 'Through the Church's being apt to hurry on too fast and too impatiently, I found myself much oppressed; especially considering my own weakness to grapple with these difficulties; this business did lye down and rise up, sleep and wake with me. It was a dismal thing to me, that I should live to see truth or peace dying or decaying in poor Cambridge.'

"But while he was, with a prudence incomparably beyond what might have been expected from a young man, managing this thorny business, he saw cause to record a passage, which perhaps will be judged worthy of some remembrance. 'That day,' writes he, (Decemb. 24, 1653,) 'after I came from him, I had a strange experience; I found hurrying and pressing suggestions against Paedobaptism, and injected scruples and thoughts whether the other way might not be right, and infant-baptism an invention of men; and whether I might with good conscience baptise children, and the like. And these thoughts were darted in with some impression, and left a strange confusion and sickliness upon my spirit. Yet, methought, it was not hard to discern that they were from the EVIL ONE. First, Because they were rather injected, hurrying suggestions, than any deliberate thoughts, or bringing any light with them. Secondly, Because they were unseasonable; interrupting me in my study for the Sabbath, and putting my spirit into a confusion, so as I had much ado to do ought in my sermon. It was not now a time to study that matter; but when in the former part of the week, I had given myself to that study, the more I studied it, the more clear and rational light I saw for Paedobaptism. But now these suggestions hurried me into scruples. But they made me cry out to God for his help ; and he did afterward calm and clear up my spirit. I thought the end of them was, First, To show me the corruption of my mind ; how apt that was to take in error, even as my heart is to take in lust. Secondly, To make me walk in fear, and take hold on Jesus Christ to keep me in the truth ; and it was a check to my former self-confidence, and it made me fearful to go needlessly to Mr. D., for methought I found a venom and poison in his insinuations and discourses against Paedobaptism. Thirdly, That I might be mindful of the aptness in others to be soon shaken in mind, and that I might warn others thereof, and might know how to speak to them from experience. And indeed my former experience of irreligious injection was some help to me to discover the nature of these.' Afterwards in the defence of the comfortable truth [the baptism of infants] he preached more than half a score ungainsayable sermons, while his own church was in some danger by the hydrophobie of anabaptism, which was come upon the mind of an eminent person in it."

Mr. Mitchell was settled over the Cambridge

church in August, 1650, when twenty-six years of age. Mather's account informs us that it was "presently" upon this, that Mr. Dunster forbore to present a child for baptism, and in that year we know his third child was born. As only "an" infant is spoken of, and this is the first mention of his withholding a child from the ordinance, the children previously borne (in 1645 and 1648) had doubtless received the "seal of the covenant." According to this account, Mr. Dunster's change of views must therefore have taken place somewhere between 1648 and 1650. But this date does not agree with a letter to friends in England,[1] now for the first time published, written, it would appear, as late as the close of 1651, in which, in answer to the question, "What do you with them that are baptized, but give no satisfactory testimony of piety when they come to age?" Mr. Dunster replied: "None of their children are baptized until one of the parents at the least do approve themselves faithful and be joined to the church. I have herewith sent you Mr. Davenport's catechism, where the question is handled, and answered according to practice."

[1] Page 287.

If the date[1] assigned to this letter is correct, Mr. Dunster held to infant baptism certainly as late as December, 1651. The conversation which Mr. Mitchell held with the President is assigned by Mather, from Mitchell's Diary, to Dec. 29, 1653, in which year also, in September or October, a fourth child was born to Mr. Dunster. But as Cotton Mather is known to have been sometimes careless in his historical statements, we are inclined to the opinion that he has here confounded two periods, and that it was the child

[1] The letter was evidently written, not only after the proclamation and crowning of Charles II. as king, in Scotland, which last event occurred on New Year's [March], 1651, but some months after the battle of Worcester, which is clearly alluded to, and which took place the 3d of September following. The letter could, therefore, hardly have been written earlier than December of that year, as the writer speaks of a proposed day of Thanksgiving for the 10th of January, which, according to Old Style, was near the end of the year. We find, indeed, no mention of such a Thanksgiving in the Colonial Records of Massachusetts, or in any history of the times, (it may have been wholly a church appointment); but the Plymouth Records (III. 5) say, that after that "crowning mercy," the battle of Worcester, "the Court desired [March 2, 1652] that a public day of thanksgiving throughout the Colony might be observed therein, to give thanks for the great victories granted to the army in behalf of the Parliament and Commonwealth of England."

born in 1653, and not the one born in 1650, that was withheld from baptism. The intense excitement consequent upon Mr. Dunster's course, and which led the pastor to visit the offending member of his flock, is placed, as we have seen, by Mitchell himself, as late as near the close of 1653. It seems hardly possible that more than two years should intervene between what was deemed so extraordinary an occurrence, as a leading preacher and the president of the College refusing baptism to his child, and the worthy pastor's attempt to allay the public excitement by seeking to recover the delinquent from his errors.[1] We are brought then to believe that the statement of Backus,[2] who was very careful as to his facts,— "Mr. Dunster boldly preached against infant baptism, and for believers' baptism, in the pulpit at Cambridge, in 1653," — is the correct one.

[1] The later date also better agrees with that of the action of the magistrates (page 119) and the Conference of Ministers and Elders, January (probably) and February, 1653, (page 120) (four or five months after the birth of Mr. Dunster's fourth child), which would naturally, in the then excited state of public feeling, be the speedy consequence of the public renunciation of infant baptism by the President of the College.

[2] History, II. 418.

It was probably, then, some time in the year 1652, that his change of views took place, the birth of a child the next year, between two or three months before Mr. Mitchell's interview with the President, affording a fitting opportunity, or creating a necessity, for the public avowal of his new views. The "sermons," in which he bore his testimony against the administration of baptism to any infant whatsoever, doubtless followed the withholding his child.

Palfrey,[1] following Mather's dates in part, suggests that Mr. Dunster, after the harsh treatment which his "*fellow-believers*" from Rhode Island, Clarke, Holmes and Crandal, had received in Massachusetts, in the year 1651, "felt self-rebuked for his silence, and that this was what prompted him to bear his testimony in some sermons." This goes upon the ground that as early at least as 1650, Mr. Dunster had become a disbeliever in infant baptism, but does not agree with Mather's statement, that the President's forbearing to present his child for baptism, and the preaching of sermons against the practice, followed immediately upon Mr. Mitchell's settlement at Cam-

[1] History, II. 398.

bridge, for it was a year and a half after that event that the three Baptists above named were visited with stripes and imprisonment. The considerations we have adduced above, especially the letter to friends in England, make it clear that his public renunciation of infant baptism must be assigned a later date. At the time of their unfortunate visit, the three strangers could not have been Mr. Dunster's "fellow-believers."

It is more likely, therefore, that the persecution of excellent Christian men, Puritans in their faith, save mainly in the one point of baptism, two of them ministers of the gospel, one of whom was an honored leader in the civil affairs of his Colony,[1] for the Christian crime of responding to

[1] Dr. John Clarke was a prominent figure in the early history of Rhode Island, and, with Roger Williams, both at home and in England, rendered invaluable services to his Colony, and to the cause of civil and religious liberty in the whole country. He was the first pastor of the Baptist Church at Newport, and was an earnest Christian. Bancroft says, that his "whole life was a continued exercise of benevolence."

Obadiah Holmes had been a member of the Congregational Church at Salem, and afterwards at Seaconck. Some years later he became a Baptist, and united with Mr. Clarke's Church at Newport, exercising his ministry in the Plymouth Colony. At Clarke's death he became pastor of the Newport Church.

the very natural invitation of an aged brother of the same belief, to visit him in Lynn, and for holding a religious service at his house, some two miles out of town, was what first aroused Mr. Dunster to seriously reconsider the whole subject of baptism. "By searching into these matters" [the above persecution], says Backus, "Mr. Dunster . . . was brought openly to renounce infant baptism."[1] We know, too, that, at that time, this ordinance was the theme of much discussion in the Colonies, and that there came near being a public controversy upon it, in Boston, between Mr. Clarke and some of his friends, and leading ministers in and around that town. Under such circumstances, an honest, independent mind, like Mr. Dunster's, who had already found reasons for considerably modifying the views of in-

John Crandall was for a time Commissioner or Deputy to the General Assembly for Newport. For a full account of the persecution, see page 301; also Backus I. ch. iv., and Clarke's "Ill Newes from New England."

"The 'place of execution' was that now occupied by the old State House. There, or in that immediate vicinity, at the head of State Street, was the Market, and near the Market stood the whipping-post." Drake's Hist. of Boston.

[1] History, I. 453.

fant baptism which he brought with him from England, would naturally be stimulated to a more thorough investigation than ever of the grounds of his belief. What his early views had been we learn from Mr. Shepard's report of his Confession of Faith.[1] "I believe," he said (probably in 1640), "that only believers and their seed ought to be received into the Church by that sacrament. . . . Concerning the outward element, something there is concerning sprinkling, in the Scriptures; hence not offended when [it] is used." Somewhat later, a quite important change of views appears from the following passage, in the "Dunster MSS.:"[2] "If parents' church-membership makes their children members, then John admitted makes his first-born a church-member; excommunicated for 7 yeares makes suppose 4 children non-members; restored in ye 9th yeare makes his 6th child a member. Show me where Christ ever indented such a covenant."

From thus separating the church-membership of infants from that of their parents, it was a natural step to deny baptism and church-member-

[1] Page 259. [2] Library of the Mass. Histor. Society.

ship to infants altogether, as was done in the "sermons" referred to above. The change of views appears to have been gradual, extending through a series of years, though hastened, no doubt, at last, by the memorable events of the summer of 1651. Mr. Dunster's subsequent reference, not only to the Scriptures, but to the works of various divines of the Reformed Church, in defence of his new views, before the Conference of Ministers (Feb. 3, 1653–4), and later, before the County Court (1657), shows that his course was the result of intelligent and deliberate research.

Having at length arrived at a settled conviction of the untenableness of infant baptism on Scriptural grounds, his next step was to conform his practice to his belief. It was here that his troubles commenced. His belief in immersion, which he seems to have held from the first, was considered no obstacle to his admission into the Cambridge Church, so long as he adhered to infant baptism[1] and would make no opposition to

[1] In the Records of the Second Church, Boston, we find this item: "1781. — The tub of the Old North Engine, then the largest in Boston, was brought into the meeting in order that a

sprinkling; for even Anabaptists[1] had been tolerated, from the first settlement of Massachusetts, in the Puritan Churches, so long as they held their peace. It was when honest convictions led to honest avowals in word and practice, that Church and State rose up to silence such impertinence of freedom.

But the public declaration of his new and, as then considered, monstrous sentiments, must

child about ten years old might, at the particular request of the mother, be baptised by immersion." Robbins' History of the Second Church.

[1] In the controversy between the Reformers, as Luther and others, and the so-called Anabaptists of their day, the question of the *mode* of baptism was not necessarily brought up. The early Anabaptists practised either immersion or sprinkling, so that for a time the mode was "unsettled and various," and to this day the Mennonites practise pouring. The English Baptists, before the 17th century, only rejected infant baptism, without insisting upon immersion, and thus "both modes were practised" together; but from the beginning of that period, immersion became the fixed mode, and, says Cutting (*Historical Vindications*, page 39), "with the greater facility, perhaps, because dipping had been preserved to about that time in the Church of England." See Evans, *Hist. of the Early English Baptists*, II. 53. The denial of infant baptism was what gave their name to the early Baptists, and made them especially obnoxious alike to Catholic and Protestant. In America, Baptists have from the first held to immersion.

have cost Mr. Dunster a severe struggle. By nature, he was opposed to controversy and strife. This appears in a letter,[1] written probably somewhat later, in which he says: "I am not utterly unacquainted with the levity and timidity of my spirit. But slender and feeble reasons they are not, or at least seem not to me, that enforce me to expose myself (that's the least), my family, and all the effects and concernments of us both, viz. the work committed to me, which, I bless God, I esteem more than myself, the peace of the church, [at Cambridge?] yea, the churches of Christ, and the tranquility of the country, which 'twere better for me to leave (though never so dear) than causelessly to hazard, and I say, expose all those." In the same strain is a letter[2] to a friend in England, written, probably, sometime earlier, in which he says: "Controversies I am unwilling to launch out into, the ocean of contention over swelling with a spring-tide, insomuch that it overflows the banks of conscience, and drowns the pleasant meadows of fruitful love, and all the sweet pastures of piety."

Such being his natural temper, the example

[1] "Dunster MSS." [2] Page 276.

of bolder spirits, such as that of his now "fellow-believers" from Rhode Island, may have helped him to take an open stand in behalf of what he was persuaded was the truth of God.

While the conflict in his mind was yet going on, he would naturally ask himself, whether it could be a godly desire for peace, and not rather a cowardly dread of persecution, that would enjoin upon him a safe silence. Others, in defence of the same views, had been willing to "endure hardness;" how could he, as a "good soldier," shrink from the trial? And he came to the conclusion that silence would be cowardice and hypocrisy; and from that moment he never swerved from his integrity. Though ever meek as a lamb, he was yet bold as a lion. Writing to the County Court in 1655, he nobly said: "I conceived then, and so do still, that I spake the truth in the feare of God, and dare not deny the same or go from it untill the Lord otherwise teach me."

CHAPTER X.

THESE opinions of Mr. Dunster being bruited about, to the "prejudice of the College and the scandal of the country," the Magistrates, or Assistants, who held nearly the same relation to the Deputies as the Senate now does to the House of Representatives, felt themselves moved to send a letter[1] to the ministers, urging them to make a thorough examination of the matter as a basis for their future action. It was probably sent soon after Mr. Mitchell's interview with the President, and was as follows:

"Reverend Sirs, The magistrates being informed that Mr. Dunster, President of the College, hath by his *practice and opinions against infant baptism* rendered himself offensive to this government, and acknowledging it their duty in respect of his relation and the trust committed to

[1] Mass. State Archives, Vol. 58.

us rightly to understand the truth of what we have heard, that accordingly we might discharge ourselves. And considering yourselves not a little concerned in this business, as ourselves together with you, whereon we are assured you will not be wanting in approving our endeavors for the preventing or *removing* of that which may tend to the prejudice of the College and scandall to the country : Think it meet to commend it to your care so to deal in this business that we may at our next meeting be thoroughly informed how the matter stands with him in respect of *his opinions*, and be thereby enabled to understand what may be expected of us, wherein not doubting of your readiness, we commend you to God and remain

Your very Loving friends."

This document bears no date, but it was doubtless prepared some time in Jan., 1653, after the interview mentioned on a previous page.[1] It was probably in response to this summons, as well as because of their own "extreme agony to rescue the good man from his mistake," that a Conference of ministers and elders was held for two

[1] Page 106.

days, Feb. 2d and 3d, 1653–4, in Boston, at which were present, besides President Dunster, nine leading ministers of Boston and vicinity, and two ruling elders[1] — twelve in all.

The thesis, proposed by Mr. Dunster, — Soli visibiliter fideles sunt baptizendi, *Visible believers only should be baptized,* — was discussed in the syllogistic method, Mr. Dunster maintaining the affirmative, and the rest the negative. This curious paper, which has never before been published, clearly exhibits Mr. Dunster's position and the grounds of it. In the course of the discussion he says: "Children under the gospel have Christ's express testimony that they have a nearer access unto him, and a nearer accept-

[1] The ministers were Mr. Wilson and Mr. Norton of Boston, Richard Mather of Dorchester, Mr. Thomson of Braintree, Mr. Allin of Dedham, John Eliot and Mr. Danforth of Roxbury, Mr. Simmes of Charlestown, Mr. Mitchell of Cambridge, and the ruling elders, Mr. Colburn and Mr. Penn. Most of these ministers had been educated in English universities, and were trained in the peculiar logic of the day. Mr. Colburn was a gentleman of great influence in Boston, and for three years was Deputy to the General Court. James Penn was also a leading man in the church and commonwealth, and one year a Deputy. Young's Chron. of Mass.

ance with him, than children under the law, viz. in Matt. 19: and Mark 10: in that when John Baptist, Christ himself and [the] Apostles did none of them baptize children, Christ, to support the spirit of parents, gave yet more express testimony than we remember to be under the law, concerning his good-will to their children in respect of that best and nearest acceptance with him, viz. their eternal salvation." "All instituted gospel worship hath some express word of Scripture. But paedobaptism hath none." [The subjects of baptism are] "only penitent believers confessing their sins. Then not infants. . . . They that cannot speak are not penitent believers confessing their sins." And when it was rejoined, that "they [infants] speak virtually," and "may be baptized in, the parents," he replied: "If we be engrafted into Christ by personal faith, then not by parental." To the proposition, "But an infant makes his covenant in his public person. An immediate parent is a public person in regard of his children, yea, in respect to a covenant bought with money, as an Indian child, that in his infancy doth *devenire in potestatem ejus*, and is his to have plenary power over him, as Abraham's servants. I say, such a one may be baptized," — to this Mr. Dunster replied, "There is now no further person but Christ for us to stand in."[1]

A letter,[2] written probably about this time, further sets forth his views upon the subject in controversy:

"That way of worship which forcibly deprives the spiritual babes and converts of the church of the due consolation from Christ and dutiful obligation to Christ — that is justly suspicious. But the baptism of unregenerate infants forcibly deprives the spiritual babes and converts of the church of their due consolation from Christ, viz.: the remission of sin &c., and dutiful obligation to Christ, viz.: to believe on him, die with him to sin, and rise to newness of life. . . . Without visible faith and repentance, they [John the Baptist and the Apostles] baptized none."

[1] The original document, (page 289) which we were permitted to copy, is in the "Dunster MSS." in the possession of the Mass. Hist. Society, to which it was presented by Miss Elizabeth Belknap, from among the papers of Dr. Belknap, the historian of New Hampshire.

[2] From the "Dunster MSS." For another extract, see page 114.

This Conference failed to "rescue the good man" (or, as Cotton Mather elsewhere calls him, the "erroneous gentleman") "from his mistake," or "to expedite the intangled out of the briars," and so, about three months after, on the 3d of May, 1654, the General Court, which, it should be remembered, was composed wholly of church-members, and was the guardian of both Church and State, passed the following significant vote:

"Forasmuch as it greatly concerns the welfare of this country that the youth thereof be educated, not only in good literature, *but sound doctrine*, this Court doth therefore commend it to *the serious consideration and special care of the Overseers of the College* and the selectmen in the several towns, *not to admit or suffer any such to be continued in the office or place of teaching*, educating, or instructing of youth or child, in *the college* or school, *that have manifested themselves unsound in the faith*, or scandalous in their lives, and not giving due satisfaction according to the rules of Christ."[1]

"I take it for granted," says Palfrey, "that

[1] Mass. Col. Rec. III. 343. IV. 182.

Dunster considered this as a blow aimed at him; for in the next month he sent in his resignation."[1] It was plain that he was guilty of more than a "mistake." He had committed an unpardonable offence. The "hope of the flock" were in peril, and his continuance in office would encourage the Baptists to still greater audacity. The theocratic leaders were, however, unwilling to assume the direct responsibility of expelling him from the College; they would make his position so uncomfortable that he would be compelled to resign. He understood their meaning, and the next month, June 10, 1654, put into the hands of the Overseers a letter addressed to the General Court, in which he said: "I here resign up the place wherein hitherto I have labored with all my heart (blessed be the Lord who gave it) serving you and yours. And henceforth (that you in the interim may be provided) I shall be willing to do the best I can for some few weeks or months to continue the work, acting according to the orders prescribed to us; if the Society in the interim fall not to pieces in our hands; and what advice for the present or

[1] Hist. New England II. 398, note.

for the future I can give for the public good, in this behalf, with all readiness of mind I shall do it, and daily by the grace of our Lord Jesus Christ, pray the Lord to help and counsel us all, in whom I rest.

"Yours faithfully to serve,

"HENRY DUNSTER."[1]

On the 25th of the same month, the Court "ungraciously" accepted his resignation, referring the case to the Overseers in the following curt style:

"In answer to a writing presented to this Court by Mr. Henry Dunster, wherein amongst other things he is pleased to make a resignation of his place as President, this Court doth order that it shall be left to the care and discretion of the Overseers of the College *to make provision, in case he persist in his resolution more than one month* (and inform the Overseers) *for some meet person to carry on and end that work for the present.*"

Neither in Mr. Dunster's letter nor in the order of the Court is there any allusion to the

[1] Mass. Col. Records III. 352.

real cause of his resignation or of their acceptance of it. The whole matter was, however, well understood by both parties; and there would be something amusing in the sort of by-play which was kept up by the Court in seeming ignorance of Mr. Dunster's crime, were it not for the heartless eagerness apparent in their action to rid the College of one whose "life" no man doubted, was "of the noblest and purest,"[1] and against whose official conduct for nearly fourteen years of toil and sacrifice no suspicion of incapacity in any sense had ever been whispered — save, of late, in the one point which covered a multitude of virtues, his honest disavowal of infant baptism.

Even now it was in Mr. Dunster's power to retain his office,[2] but it was upon a condition to

[1] Palfrey.

[2] Hubbard, a graduate of the College in 1642, says in his History: "His body was solemnly interred at Cambridge, where he had spent the choise part of his studies and of his life, and *might there have continued*, if he had been endowed with that wisdom which many others have wanted besides himself, *to have kept his singular opinion to himself*, when there was little occasion of venting thereof," — a confession more creditable to Hubbard as an historian than as a Christian and Christian minister.

which he could not submit, though it was urged upon him by the Overseers — that he refrain from "imposing" his opinions upon others. Simple silence — that was all. Only one thing stood in the way, — he was an honest man. What he believed, that he must speak. God's truth, as he conceived it, was to be published, not concealed. The work at Cambridge was dear to him, he had "labored" in it "with all his heart;" but he could lay it down, rather than wound his conscience or dishonor God. And so, knowing the consequences of his action, about a month after the reference by the General Court to the Overseers, of his letter of resignation, with an involved condition, he again bore public testimony in the Church at Cambridge, on Sunday, against infant baptism. He probably felt that, under the circumstances, silence would be construed into a confession of error, and submission to the understood terms of continuance in office. Doubtless, too, in the excited state of public feeling, when "the brethren of the Church were somewhat vehement and violent in their signifying of their dissatisfaction," Mr. Dunster's every act and word would be watched with eagle eyes. He must therefore re-affirm his honest convictions, be the consequences what they might.

But it is not in the Church records that we find an account of his "testimony" at this time, but in those of the County Court, held at Cambridge. The record is as follows:—

"At a County Court held at Cambridge the 3^{d} of the 2^{d} m. [April],[1] 1655.[2]

Mr. Henry Dunster being presented to this Court by the Grand Jury for disturbance of the ordinances of Christ uppon the Lord's daye at Cambridge July the 30th, 1654, to the dis-

[1] According to the Old Style, the year began in March.

[2] Quincy (*Hist. of Cambridge Col. p.* 18), says: "Indicted by the grand jury for disturbing the ordinance of infant baptism in the Cambridge Church, convicted by the Court, sentenced to a public admonition on lecture day, and laid under bonds for good behavior, Dunster's martyrdom was consummated by being compelled in Oct., 1654, to resign his office of President, and to throw himself on the tender mercies of the General Court."

He appears to have been deceived as to the order of events, by the fact that the offence for which Mr. Dunster was tried in the County Court, was *committed* prior to his resignation; but the trial and conviction did not occur till about eight months after the offence, and about six months after his resignation.

honor of the name of Christ his truth and minister.

Severall witnesses tendered to attest uppon their oathes respectively, that uppon the Lords daye July the 30[h] 1654, Mr. Henry Dunster spake to the congregation in the time of the publique ordinance to the interruption thereof without leave, which was also aggravated in that he being desired by the Elder to forbeare, and not to interrupt an ordinance of Christ, yet notwithstanding he proceeded in way of complaint to the Congregation, saying, I am forbidden to speake that in Christ's name which I would have testified. And in his following speeches he asserted as his testimony in the name of Christ these things:

1. That the subjects of Baptisme were visible pennitent believers, and they only by vertue of any rule, example, or any other light in the new testament.

2. That there was an action now to be done, which was not according to the institution of Christ.

3. That the exposition as it had been held forth was not the mind of Christ.

4. That the covenant of Abraham is not a ground for Baptisme no not after the institution thereof.

5. That there were such corruptions[1] stealing into the Church, which every faithful Christian ought to beare witnes against.

[1] Mr. Dunster probably had reference to a tendency which had begun to show itself, in the opinion of many of the best men, towards impairing the purity of the churches; a tendency which clearly revealed itself in the synods of 1657 and 1662, in what was afterwards called "the half-way covenant," according to which persons of blameless life, though, as unregenerated, not deemed fit for church-membership, were allowed to have their children baptized, on condition of their "owning" the covenant made by their parents for them in their infancy. President Chauncy, Increase Mather (at first), Mr. Davenport, and others strongly opposed this broad departure from the original stricness of the churches, fearing that "the sacred ordinance of baptism would come to be applied to such unmeet subjects as would in a while put an end to New England's primitive and peculiar glory of undefiled administration." Mr. Dunster foresaw this danger, but would avoid it by rejecting infant baptism altogether, and confining baptism to believers. He also, says Uhden, "rejected infant baptism, manifestly for the sake of carrying out consistently the Congregationalist principle; for the sacraments being in his view of equal rank, he held the same prerequisites necessary for both." *The New England Theocracy.* By H. F. Uhden. Translated by Mr. H. C. Conant, 1859. See page 110 of this work.

The Court ordered that Mr. Henry Dunster according to the Eclesiast. Law, page 19,[1] at the next lecture at Cambridge should (by such magistrate as should then be present) be publiquely admonished and give bond for his good behavior.

Mr. Henry Dunster acknowledged that he had spoaken theis particulars above named, and said that he owned them, and that he would stand by them, in the feare of God, and after farther debate, he gave in his Answer in writing, as followeth,

Aprill 4th, 1655. I answer to the presentment of the Grand Jury.

[1] "Forasmuch as the open contempt of God's word and messengers thereof is the desolating sin of civil State and Churches: It is ordered, that if any Christian (so called) within this jurisdiction shall contemptuously behave himself towards the word preached or the messengers thereof called to dispense, either by interrupting him in his preaching, or by charging him falsely with any error which he hath not taught in the open face of the church, or like a son of Korah, cast upon his true doctrine or himself any reproach to the honor of the Lord Jesus who hath sent him, and to the disparagement of his holy ordinance, and making God's ways contemptible and ridiculous: that every such person or persons (whatever censure the Church may pass) shall for the first scandal be convented and reproved openly by the magistrate at some lecture, and bound to their good behaviour." 1646. Charters and General Laws of the Colony of Mass.

I Answer first, that I am not conscious that I did anything contemptuously or in the open contempt of Gods word or messengers, and therefore I am not guilty of the breach of that lawe pag. 19, as I conceive.

For the particulars that were charged against mee, the termes or expressions wherein they are presented to the Honored Court I owne not, being not accurately the same that were spoaken, especially the 1st, 4th and 5th, but the matter or purport of them I spake. I also acknowledged and do, that for the manner they were not seasonably spoaken, but for the matter, I conceived then, and so do still, that I spake the truth in the feare of God, and dare not deny the same or go from it untill the Lord otherwise teach me, and this I pray the Honored Court to take for mine Answer.

As for any words or expressions that in mixed or broken conference, interrogations by sundry persons propounded, and mine Answers, interrupted before they have been fully expressed, I Heartily and Humbly pray you, mine Honored Judges, as you desire to find mercy with the gracious Judge the Lord Jesus Christ, that you wilbe pleased to give the most candid and Christian Construction if any were amisse, seeing Charity thinketh no Evill, and seeing by Interruptions they were not perfected, and especially seeing since my sicknes yesternight, my mind and expressions are not in a Capacity to be so cleere and distinct as usually. That therefore no lapse in expression proceeding from the aforesaid grounds, or meere naturall infirmity may be improved against your Humble Servant and afflicted Brother,

HENRY DUNSTER."

This trial, for the alleged offence of disturbing the public worship, but for the real crime of believing and avowing an opinion, took place about eight months after the offence was committed, and when the offender was no longer President. The Overseers, however, did not wait so long. Cotton Mather probably refers to this period, when he says: "Mr. Henry Dunster continued the President of Harvard College until his unhappy entanglements in the snares of anabaptism filled the Overseers with uneasy fears lest the students by his means should come to be ensnared; which uneasiness was at length *so suggested* to him, that on October 24th, 1654, he presented unto the Overseers an instrument under his hands, wherein he resigned his presidentship, and they accepted his resignation."[1]

Certainly the Overseers, to whose "care and discretion" Mr. Dunster's resignation had been referred June 25, 1654, could no longer stand in doubt. Mr. Dunster was past hope of recovery from the "briars," and so, not long after the scene in the church at Cambridge, July 30th, they proceeded to inform the President that the interests of the College and Colony required his removal. Mr. Dunster, on his part, could no longer doubt the intentions of the rulers in church and state, and a second time, Oct. 24th, 1654, he sent his resignation — a final one — to the Overseers. He still occupied the President's house, but his connection with the College, in the interest of which he had labored with singular disinterestedness and fidelity during fourteen years, had ceased. The troubler in the Puritan

[1] Magnalia.

Israel was " driven " from his post of influence, — driven for an opinion.[1]

One of his successors in office, Josiah Quincy, says in this connection: " Dunster would never have been compelled to resign had not his excited zeal for his own sectarian faith led him, in a moment of indiscretion, to overstep the bounds of prudence, and to bear public testimony, in the church at Cambridge, against infant baptism." That is, in other words, had Mr. Dunster, in the exercise of common discretion, kept his new opinions to himself, he might have retained his place in the College.

It is, doubtless, true that silence would have saved him his office, but to keep silence under present circumstances was just what, as a Christian man, he was incapable of doing. Granted that he did not select the most fitting time and place for his public testimony; so much Mr. Dunster himself was willing to concede. And it is certainly possible that some other occasion might have been more " seasonable,"

[1] That it was solely for this reason is plain from the language of Cotton Mather. See page 103 of this work; also page 127, note.

especially for himself, inasmuch as he did in a sense, "interrupt" the ordinary service of the Sabbath, and render himself liable, according to the current rigid construction of the laws against heresy, to the charge of casting reproach upon an ordinance of the gospel; but had he not spoken at this time, he must have done so at some other. It was not with him a choice between the concealment or the declaration of his sentiments, but a simple question of when and where he should speak. So that it was not an imprudent avowal of his opinions in church on the Lord's day which cost him his place, but his openly declaring them at all. The theocracy would have been just as much offended by any other public testimony against infant baptism. It was his standing to his opinions that was his unpardonable sin.

It is, then, we think, unwarrantable language, to say that Mr. Dunster's "excited zeal for his own sectarian faith led him in a moment of indiscretion to overstep the bounds of prudence." His "sectarian faith" was to him the truth of God, which, with patience and prayer, he had sought after, and which he "dare not deny." His whole life is proof that he was a man of an eminently catholic and charitable spirit. But he was as positive in his convictions, as catholic in his temper. God's truth was "more sweet to him than anything else in the world." And certainly his own view of the case, — given after a night's opportunity for calm reflection, — that he had spoken "the truth in the fear of God," is entitled to great weight.

At the time he bore this "public testimony," the subject of his continuance in office was still pending, — made contingent upon his consent to silence, — and he must consequently have desired to clearly define his position. Had he refrained from any public avowal of his obnoxious sentiments, it might have seemed that he was seeking to conciliate the authorities for the sake of office. It was therefore indispensable that he should publickly commit himself — either to forbear to "disseminate or publish" his peculiar tenets, as was required of his successor, or, what alone was possible in his case, to refuse to yield to any compromise. Another day and place than what he selected might indeed have answered his purpose; except that perhaps the more public the occasion, the better might all understand just where he stood. And, as the point at issue was an ecclesiastical one, there seemed a special propriety in his making his remarks in the church.

Those remarks, as we have seen, settled the question of his connection with the College, and accordingly, about three months after this open declaration of opinions, his resignation became a necessity. He had not come to the prescribed terms, and was compelled to vacate his office.

It is wrong, and hurtful to the moral sense of the community to stigmatize such rare conscientiousness as sectarian indiscretion. Rather should it be held up to universal admiration. Mr. Dunster by this sort of indiscretion became one of the pioneers in the cause of human freedom.

Nine days after his resignation, at a meeting of "the Honorable and Reverend Overseers of the College," the following action was taken :

"Mr. Mather [Richard] and Mr. Norton are desired by the Overseers of the College to tender unto the Rev. Mr. Charles Chauncy the place of President, with the stipend of £100 per annum, . . . and withal to signify to him that it is expected and desired that he *forbear to disseminate or publish any tenets concerning the necessity of immersion in baptism, and celebration of the Lord's Supper at evening, or to oppose the received doctrines therein.*"[1]

[1] Quincy, I. 467. Mr. Chauncy believed in infant baptism, but by immersion. The Plymouth Church held him in such high esteem for his learning and pastoral gifts, that in 1639 or 1640, in order to secure his services, they proposed that he and his colleague, Mr. Rayner, should baptize each according to his own views. But he was unwilling to accede to the terms, and accepted a call to Scituate, where more freedom would be allowed him. Had he been as pliable in 1640 as he proved to be in 1654, he would have remained at Plymouth, and that Colony might perhaps have had a rival College, with himself for its first President. This would appear from a letter of Edward Winslow to John Winthrop, in 1640, in which the writer says: "I suppose you have heard what was the issue of the day of humiliacion concerning the election of Mr. Chauncy. But things are like to goe ill, for on the 2d day of this week a mocon was made by Mr. Paddy and some that inordinately cleave to him, for his settling at Jones River, some three miles from Plymouth, who purposeth there *to lay the foundacon of an Academy*, and reade the arts to some that are fitt for that purpose, soe that they also may have use of his gifts. I manifested my dislike to the Governor [Bradford], who still pressed his gifts, but I told him they must still retaine his errors etc. with his gifts, which were like to weaken if not destroy both the Congregacions of Plymouth and Duxburrow, being situated in the midst equally between both." IV. Hist. Col. VI. 169.

To say nothing of the almost indecent haste with which a pre-arranged plan[1] is consummated, what honorable mind does not confess the vast moral superiority of the out-going over the in-coming President ; the former refusing to retain an office which necessitated the denial of his belief, the other accepting that same office on the express condition of silence ? Was it " indis-

[1] On the very day of Mr. Dunster's resignation, Oct. 24th, the Overseers "agreed that the Rev. Mr. Richard Mather and the Rev. Mr. John Norton speak with the Rev. Mr. Chauncy, and, as they shall see cause, encourage him to accept of an invitation to the presidency of the College, in case the Overseers give him a call thereto." One would like to know whether Mr. Dunster had formally signified his resignation to the Overseers, when this action was taken. Had he done so, we should suppose some note of it would have been made in the records of the meeting. But no matter ; Mr. Dunster's removal was a foregone conclusion.

Nov. 2d, a Committee was appointed to tender to Mr. Chauncy the place of President, and on the 27th of the same month, being a month after Mr. Dunster's resignation, the services of inauguration took place.

It is interesting to note Roger Williams' allusion to this event, in a letter to John Winthrop Jr. : "Mr. Dunster (as is said) expecting to be outed about his judgment of children's baptisme, withdrew himself, and Mr. Chancie, who was shipt for England, is now master of the Colledge." Winthrop Papers, Histor. Coll.

cretion" in Mr. Dunster and "prudence" in Mr. Chauncy that produced these opposite conclusions? Mr. Quincy himself shall answer, when, speaking of the latter, he says: "He seems . . . not to have possessed the stern, uncompromising, self-sacrificing spirit which characterized his predecessor." This is a true record.

Mr. Peirce, a respected historian of the College, says of the controversy on baptism: "Fortunately it is a matter on which little depends; . . . the substance of Christianity is of infinitely higher importance than this form of expressing our devotion to it, and that a controversy which cannot be settled had better be dropped."[1] Of course the "substance" is higher than a "form," but by so summary a process Mr. Dunster's, or any man's, earnest opinions about the doctrine of baptism cannot be set down as sectarian trifling, or, as Mr. Quincy has it, as a proof of "fanaticism." Mr. Dunster did not differ from his brethren for "slight reasons."[2] Whether right or wrong in his views of the ordinance, as to its mode or subjects, he thought he saw corruptions

[1] History of Harvard College, Appendix, page 36.

[2] Page 117.

stealing into the Church through the perversion of this ordinance, in which point others of high standing in the Church, who still held to infant baptism, were agreed with him. He regarded the question of the proper subjects of baptism — which widely agitated the churches of New England in his day — as vital to the true idea of Christianity as a spiritual system and the Church as a spiritual body, and as also involving the very authority of Jesus Christ. It is not our province in this volume to pronounce upon the correctness of his opinions, but we may clear him from the charge of narrow sectarianism and fanaticism. Mr. Dunster was a man who did his own thinking, and with whom to believe was to act. And so he suffered for conscience' sake. Let such suffering be honored. Mr. Quincy speaks of Dunster's "martyrdom." Surely that is too honorable a word for a sectarian zealot.

CHAPTER XI.

THE world was now before Mr. Dunster, but his prospects were far from encouraging. Besides himself, he had a wife and children to provide for. There was no other College in the land to seek the benefit of his profound learning; the churches regarded him as a heretic, an Anabaptist, "that bugbear of New England," a disturber of the peace of Zion and of the Commonwealth; and what church would desire, or if it desired, would dare [1] to invite his

[1] In 1653 the General Court enacted, "That every person that shall publish or maintain any heterodox or erroneous doctrine shall be liable to be questioned and censured by the County Court where he liveth, according to the merit of his offence." Col. Rec. IV. 151. It is probable that this action was prompted by Mr. Dunster's course, and was aimed directly at him.

services, though he had the reputation of being "an orthodox preacher of the truths of Christ, very powerful through his blessing to move the affection"? Thus, regarded everywhere with suspicion, while everywhere acknowledged to be a man of incorruptible integrity and eminent ability, whither should he direct his steps, and what should be his employment? In his embarrassment, he sent, eleven days after his resignation, a Petition to the General Court, in which with singular meekness but without servility, without receding a step from his avowed belief, he invoked their merciful consideration of his circumstances:

"The Petition of Henry Dunster in case of important and importunate exigencies humbly sheweth:

"With all thankfulnesse acknowledging your forbearance to take advantage at his resignation of his place June the last past untill your humble petitioner might have conference with the honored and Reverend Overseers about the grievances him afflicting, by which your humble petitioner, being enformed to some measure of satisfaction, in submissive willingnesse re-assumed his place and answerably, ever since, to his power dutifully demain'd himselfe therein untill the 24 of the 8th month [October] last, when upon the prudent and peaceable motions of the said honored and Reverend Overseers for the publique weal of the Society, concurring with other reasons your humble petitioner thereunto inducing, he your said petitioner peaceably laid down and resign'd his place again the second time in such wise and manner as might be of best report and most inoffensive to all sides.

"Therefore your humble petitioner submissively desireth that it may neither be thought, nor by any of your honored selves reported, that your said petitioner did cast off his place out of any froward morosity, foolish levity, or ingratefull despising either of the Court's forbearance or the Overseers' amicable conferences, for all the Honored and Reverend Overseers can beare witnesse to the contrary, and how this thing was transacted, composedly by their motives and arguments concurring with your humble petitioner's conceptions and acceptation.

"Moreover it is your said petitioner's humble request that the honored Court would be pleased to take into their Christian consideration the grounds and reasons whereupon the late honored Committee for the College commended to your Court the equity of allowance to be made to your humble petitioner for his extraordinary labor in, about, and concerning the weal of the College over and beside his dayly employment in the education of youth for the space of these fourteen yeares last past, that your humble petitioner may be enabled thereby to discharge his debts in Old and New England.

"And whereas your humble petitioner with singular industry thorow great difficultyes erected the house wherein for the present he dwelleth, it is his humble desire that he may peacably enjoy the same, untill all accounts due to him from ye Corporation be orderly and valuably to him your humble petitioner satisfyed and pay'd.

"And whereas your humble petitioner, being a free man of this Colony, doth not only by vertue of his oath, but also, from an innate love and affection, ever hath and still doth seek the weal and felicity thereof in all things according to his best light and with his whole person, property and estate, and soe teacheth all his to doe that noe member of this Colony may be uselesse or unprofitable; therefore it is your petitioner's humble desire for his account's sake one day to be made to God of the talents to him betrusted, for the maintenance of his afflicted family (which the light of nature teacheth infidels), for the weal of this plantation which it is written in your servant's heart to promote; that therefore according to his education and abilityes, without all impeachment, molestation, or discountenance from the authority of this colony, he your said humble servant, walking piously and peacably, may seek further and vigorously prosecute the spiritual or temporall weal of the inhabitants thereof in preaching the Gospel of Christ, teaching or training up of youth, or in any other laudable or liberall caling as God shall chalk out his way, and when, and where, and in what manner he shall find acceptance. . . .

"Yours to his power in all things humbly to serve.

HENRIE DUNSTER.

"4. 9ber [November] 54 [1654]."

To this petition the Court replied as follows: [1]

"1. In answer to that section, figure 1. What extraordinary labor in, about, and concerning the weal of the College, for the space of fourteen years we know of none, but what was the President's duty belonging to his place; unless he can show the particulars of these labors which were extraordinary.

"2. In answer to the second. It is most unreasonable. For he may protract the making up of his accounts some years, and thereby hinder the comfortable being of him who is chosen to the work of the College. What the President can make justly to appear to be his due, it must bee paid him with convenient speed.

"3. This Court doth not think it meet, for reasons (whereof Mr. Dunster is not ignorant), and well known to this Court, to grant this part of the petition. What other laudable or liberal calling, besides preaching and education of youth, is intended, Mr. Dunster is to explain himself. . . .

"Agreed on by the Magistrates, with further reference to our brethren, the Deputies.

R. BELLINGHAM, Governor."

[1] State Archives, vol. 58, 26.

Quincy says that Mr. Dunster's "appeal to their humanity and justice" was treated in a "heartless way." The government seems to have been in no mood favorable to a proper consideration of his claims upon their generosity or justice. What they must do they will do; nothing more. Instead of magnanimously acknowledging his "extraordinary" services, they indelicately require him to "show the particulars." Instead of graciously according him a few weeks or months in which to make up his accounts, they seem only anxious to hurry him off the College premises. Instead of treating him as an honorable man, they regard him with suspicion. He must have some sinister purpose in what he had suggested about a "laudable or liberal calling;" let him "explain" himself. To his appeal for an open opportunity to serve God and the Commonwealth, and in behalf of his "afflicted family," the Court has no friendly word. For "reasons well-known" to them, which of course are neither more nor less than his opinions about baptism, they will reduce him to hard conditions. He shall have no opportunity to use his talents or earn his bread within their jurisdiction.

Plainly, their object is to drive him from the Colony, as they had done from the College. They certainly do not want him to teach their youth, nor to preach ; what other "liberal" profession is left to him ? It must be that he intends to be a lawyer, a profession held in detestation and dread by our Puritan fathers. One limb of the law had been worried out of Boston ; another must not be permitted to start up in his place. Who could tell what deep designs he might have in mind against the theocracy ? As a lawyer he might endeavor to employ the Charter,[1] the laws of England and

[1] "From 1640 to 1660 they [the people of Massachusetts Colony] approached very near to an independent Commonwealth, and during this period completed a system of laws and government, the plan of which they had before laid and begun to execute. In this they departed from their Charter, and instead of making the laws of England the groundwork of their code, they preferred the laws of Moses &c." Hutchinson, Hist. Mass. II. 11. Capt. Cudworth, an eminent Plymouth magistrate, deposed for his tolerant views, about the year 1658, expressing, while disapproving, the opinions of the ruling party at that time, wrote : "If we can but keep the people ignorant of their liberties and privileges, then we have liberty to act in our own wills what we please."

"I know not how," says Hutchinson, "to excuse the persecution of all who would not conform to their religious establish-the established rights of Englishmen, to work trouble among them. The Puritans of that day were trained logicians, and they well knew the logical results of Mr. Dunster's theological heresy. And when we consider the political and ecclesiastical dogmas which held sway at that time in New England, and the excited state of public feeling at the aberrations of one who was President of the College and a leading member of the Church, we cannot regard these considerations as puerile. A man who had taken the stand that Mr. Dunster had done — what might he not do?

It must be remembered, too, that the government was now under the leadership of Bellingham and Endicott, who for years divided the highest and next highest honors of the Colony

ments, when their Charter granted toleration to all Christians except Papists."

Lawyers, it was perhaps feared, might insist too strongly upon following the common law and the Statutes of England, and oppose leaving so much to the "good sense" and "discretion of the Court." See page 33. For, as Hon. Joel Parker (Lowell Lectures, 1869) says, by way of apology, "The Puritans claimed the right to pass their own laws, with the Bible, and not the common law, as their fundamental law."

between them, the one or the other being Governor or Lieutenant-Governor. These men, though they rendered great services to the country, were yet stern and intolerant.[1] Bellingham's "acerbity of character," as was shown in his "factious opposition to Winthrop," was especially conspicuous, and he was now Governor. It is easy to trace his hand in all these proceedings against Dunster.

The "heartless" treatment which his "Petition" had met with from the General Court, did not prevent Mr. Dunster from sending to the same body, within six days, Nov. 10th, the following "Considerations,"[2] intended chiefly as a reply to that part of the Court's response to his "Petition," in which his request to remain a while in the President's house had been dismissed as "most unreasonable:"

"1st. The time of the year is unseasonable, being now very near the shortest day, and the depth of winter.

[1] Savage (note to Winthrop's Journ.) says that "Endicott [and Dudley also] was less mild than Winthrop."

[2] State Archives, vol. 58, 30.

2d. The place unto which I go is unknown to me and my family, and the ways and means of subsistence, to one of my talents and parts, or for the containing or conserving my goods, or disposing of my cattle, accustomed to my place of residence.

3d. The place from which I go, hath fire, fuel, and all provisions for man and beast, laid in for the winter. To remove some things will be to destroy them; to remove others, as books and household goods, to hazard them greatly. The house I have builded, upon very damageful conditions to myself, out of love for the College, taking country pay in lieu of bills of exchange on England, or the house would not have been built; and a considerable part of it was given me, at my request, out of respect to myself, albeit for the College.

4th. The persons, all besides myself, are women and children, on whom little help, now their minds lie under the actual stroke of affliction and grief. My wife is sick, and my youngest child extremely so, and hath been for months, so that we dare not carry him out of doors, yet much worse now than before. However, if a place be found, that may be comfortable for them, and reasonably answer the obstacles above mentioned, myself will willingly bow my neck to any yoke of personal self-denial, for I know for what and by whom, by grace, I suffer. . . .

5th. The state of the Colledg Requireth my residence untill all accounts be made up, ballanced and allowed. That the Honored Overseers and Corporation may know in what estate I leave the Colledg de facto. That afterward there may be no uncomfortable complaints or offence on either side unless the Honored Overseers and Corporation accept my accounts given in already to the end of the year 1652, and so acquiess.

2ly. My residence is required in reference to the Reverend President elected, that I may show him what our way hath been, particularly seeing Mr. Okes [Oakes] [1] and all long resident fellows are gone away, and others in the country have long discontinued and know not the present state of the Colledg.

3. In reference to the servants of the house, to regulate all their accounts and declare their work to the president elect.

[1] Urian Oakes, afterwards President of the College.

6. What place near the Colledg can be found, is more convenient by far for the Reverend President elect, who is in a moveable posture, than for me on that account.

2ly. Because myself for sundry years was compelled to what inconvenience can befall him though but for a few months, before your desires be accomplished.

7. The whole transaction of this business is such, which in process of time, when all things come to mature consideration, may very probably create grief on all sides; yours subsquent, as mine antecedent. I am not the man you take me to be. Neither if you knew what I hould, [hold] and why, can I persuade myself that you would act, as I am at least tempted to think you do? But our times are in God's hands, with whom all sides hope, by grace in Christ, to find favor, which shall be my prayer for you, as for myself,

Who am, honored gentlemen, yours to serve,

HENRY DUNSTER."

The "simple, touching pathos"[1] of this appeal

[1] Quincy.

was not without its effect. Mr. Dunster was allowed to remain in the President's house till the following March, the beginning of 1655. But in nothing else does the Court abate its severity.

It is observable that in this second communication Mr. Dunster renews only one request which he had made in the first, — he begs a temporary shelter for his family. He appears before the Court as the tender husband and father, pleading that his wife and little ones, the oldest but nine, and the youngest but four years old, besides some of the children of his former wife who were under his care, may not be driven out homeless in mid-winter. He has no other favor to ask ; and to the suspicions of the Court as to his future course, he only replies in the simple language of conscious integrity, " I am not the man you take me to be."

Nothing but parental tenderness could have forced the retiring President to present himself before the Court a second time in the character of a petitioner. He was evidently as gentle as he was conscientious. The necessities of those who looked up to him as their protector overcame the natural promptings of pride. And as a Christian, he felt that he was in "God's hands," and he meekly bowed his head to the stroke. It is plain that there is no revenge in his heart. He still clings to his brethren, though they cast him off. They treat him coldly because they do not understand him. "Neither if you knew what I hold, and why, can I persuade myself that you would act, as I am at least tempted to think you do." By and by they will judge him more intelligently and righteously. Meanwhile, he nobly adds, "All sides hope by grace in Christ, to find favor" with God. And with a prayer for his persecutors — his deluded brethren — he bids them adieu.

What but a profound conviction of the correctness of his views upon the point in controversy, and an unswerving loyalty to truth, could have nerved such a man, so gentle and genial, to brave the terrors of the theocratic rule?

But Mr. Dunster was not permitted to spend in peace even the brief respite granted him by the General Court till March. A little more than two months after his second petition, he was summoned, as we have seen,[1] before the

[1] Page 129.

County Court, in Cambridge, on the 3d of the 2d month [April], 1655, to answer to a charge relating to an offence committed some eight months before. As this trial belongs to this period of our narrative, we here refer to it again. And here Mr. Richard Bellingham, who was soon to give place to Mr. Endicott, as Governor, appears as one of the Justices on the occasion, with Increase Nowell, Capt. Humphrey Atherton, and Major Simon Willard, Mr. Dunster's brother-in-law, all men of note, as associates on the bench. These, with the fourteen members of the Grand Jury, by whom Mr. Dunster was indicted, were all church-members, some of them, no doubt, members with him of the church at Cambridge. The "severall witnesses" who "tendered to attest" to his offence, must also have been his "brethren;" for who outside the church would care to appear against him in such a matter? Thus Mr. Dunster was judged by "the saints," and not by "unbelievers"! But why then treat *him* as an "infidel," and not as a brother? Why arraign him before the Court instead of the Church? Were his opponents afraid to meet him in argument? They were at least reluctant to do so;

for if the pastor, "the matchless" Mitchell, was "fearfull to go needlessly to Mr. Dunster," finding, as he thought, "a venom and a poison in his insinuations and discourses against paedobaptism," as "from the Evil One," who could safely listen to the artful words of this emissary of Satan? The arm of the law shall be invoked to silence him and disgrace him. And so the same set of men, who dared not meet him with texts and syllogisms, cowardly and cruelly sought to undermine his character and influence. But why not be satisfied with his dismissal from the College and his removal from the College grounds, which must have already taken place, it being now past the time granted him by the Court (March, 1655)? It is hardly assuming too much to suppose that this crowning insult was instigated by Bellingham,[1] to make sure Mr. Dunster's

[1] Hawthorne, in *The Scarlet Letter*, represents Gov. Bellingham as "naturally stern," and of an "aspect" "rigid and severe," which is perfectly true to the facts of his character. But while prompt to punish others for violations of the law, even of an intolerant one, he was not above the meanness of resorting to a trick to relieve himself from a merited penalty; for "his wife having died, in 1641 he married a second time, and performed the marriage ceremony himself. He was prosecuted for a viola-

exodus, not only from the College and the President's house, but from Cambridge, where his presence would be fraught with peril to the students and the Church. The people, who, as Mather tells us, were so "vehement and violent" against their heterodox brother, could easily be persuaded, if they needed any urging, to bring a suit against him. And so, when he could scarcely have got over the care of providing a new home for his family, he was arraigned before the County Court, among men charged with adultery and other immoralities, to answer for a crime — so it was called — committed nearly a year before! Evidently his enemies would allow him no rest or peace.

What a spectacle, on that 3d day of April, 1655! He who had lived among them for fourteen years a beloved neighbor, the honored head of the College, the expounder to them on many occasions of the Word of God, and for a season their acting pastor, — a man of pure life and unblemished reputation, now arraigned as a criminal,

tion of the law, but at the trial he refused to leave the bench, but sat, and tried himself, and thus escaped all punishment." Amer. Cyclopedia.

charged with "contemptuous carriage towards God's word and messenger;" and all because, in his spiritual home, among his brethren and friends, he had frankly stated his objections to a certain doctrine and practice of the church. And what a spectacle, when, on lecture-day, this learned, pious, venerable man was admonished, before the congregation, by one of the magistrates. This was to give the solemn sanction of the Church to the civil sentence. As a church they had feared to try him, but they could say Amen to the decision of the Court. It is to be hoped, for the honor of human nature, that all the congregation did not share the vehemence of his accusers, or that their animosity relented as they looked upon the meek sufferer. Some, no doubt, secretly sympathized with him, and perhaps some even dared to risk the hazard of expressing, at least to him, their disapproval of the proceedings.

To the lot of which one of the magistrates for that year it fell, to administer the "admonition," we are not informed. One would suppose that Mr. Dunster's noble defence in his letter to the Court the day after the trial would have quite disarmed his persecutors, or at least made the reading to him a public lecture an unpleasant task. Certainly Major Willard, the ex-president's brother-in-law, would hardly wish to face the duty as a magistrate, which he had imposed as a judge.

We here introduce, though it occurred nearly two years later, another prosecution of Mr. Dunster. In the year 1656 (Dec. 29th), a daughter (Elisabeth) was born to him; and as, within the following three months, he failed to present it for baptism, Moses and Aaron again fell to "kissing each other" over this repeated disregard of an ordinance of the gospel. The inquisition commenced by the action of the grand jury, at Cambridge, on the 7th of April, 1657, and was then taken up by the next County Court, meeting at Charlestown, on the 16th of June following. There were present on the Bench, Governor Endicott, Deputy Governor Bellingham, Capt. Dan. Gookin,[1] Major Simon Willard and Major Humph. Atherton. The Court record is as follows: —

[1] Daniel Gookin resided at Cambridge. "He is characterized as a man of good understanding, rigid in his religious and political principles, but of exemplary piety &c." Holmes' Hist. of Cambridge. Hist. Col. II. Ser. VII. 23.

"Mr. Henry Dunster, being summoned to answer the presentment of the Grand Jury at Cambridge,[1] April 7, 1657, for not bringing his child to the Holy Ordinance of baptisme, and also for neglecting to appear according to former summons, appeared in Court and made his Answer thereunto, pleading that he could not do it in faith, as all well knew, and also naming divers Authors* concerning that poynt, affirmed that none of them had given any demonstrative argument touching infant baptism, but had left the same in medio probabile, but in after discourse being charged with the falcenes of his assercc̄on therein by the Government, he answered (waveing his positive assertion) and said it was so to his conscience. The Court sollemly admonished him of his dangerous error, and ordered that he should give bond for his appearance at the next Court of Assistants at Boston.

* Calvin, Ames, Hooker and some others.

---

[1] Though Mr. Dunster had removed to Scituate (see page 202), he must have retained his civil connection in some sort with Massachusetts, as we find him here summoned before a Massachusetts Court. As he had property to look after in this Colony, he probably spent a portion of his time at Cambridge and vicinity.

"Mr. Henry Dunster acknowledgeth himself indebted unto Mr. Richard Russell, Treasurer, ten pounds sterling well and truly to be paid by him, his heires, executors, and administrators, upon condition that he will appear at the next Court of Assistants to be held at Boston, in September next, then and there to answer the presentment of the Grand Jury at Cambridge, April 7, 1657."[1]

With reference to the two trials before the County Court, it may be said, that the Grand Jury in presenting Mr. Dunster, and the judges in condemning him, only acted under the law of 1646, and that he had no just cause of com-

[1] No record remains of further proceedings. Thomas Gould (see pages 87 and 98) was a fellow-sufferer with Mr. Dunster at this Court. The Record reads: "Thomas Goold being presented by the Grand Jury held at Cambridge, April 7, 1657, for not bringing his child to the holy ordinance of baptism, the said Goold appearing in Court confessed his child to be unbaptized, the Court sollemly admonished him of his dangerous error.

Thomas Goold being again called the 24: (4) 57, [24th June, 1657] and not appearing, the Court ordered that the Clarke of the Court should send an attachment for him to appear before any magistrate in case he did not refuse upon notice given him to give twenty pounds bond for his appearance at the next Court of Assistants at Boston, and that he should pay the costs of Court."

plaint. He had violated a known law, and exposed himself to its penalty.

If the law in question is to be interpreted by the spirit of the times, he was doubtless guilty. That spirit was one of intolerance, and was disposed to regard any open denial of infant baptism, however calmly and candidly made, as an "open contempt of God's word." The jury and the justices, as certainly did the prime instigators of the prosecution, doubtless shared in this general feeling. But Mr. Dunster, no more prejudiced on one side than were his prosecutors on the other, may be presumed to have been as capable of understanding the true meaning of the statute as any other man; and, persuaded of the purity of his motives in what he had said and done, he said to the Court: "I am not conscious that I did any thing contemptuously or in open contempt of God's word or messengers, and therefore I am not guilty of the breach of that law, page 19, as I conceive."

It should be further considered, that though it was not customary for any one to follow the preaching with remarks, on the Sabbath day, yet the privilege of doing so, at least on rare occasions, might, it would seem, have been conceded to one who had so long been an honored member of the church, who had preached before it many times, and who, after Mr. Shepard's death, had been its acting pastor till the appointment of a successor. It was surely no great offence for such a man to occupy a few moments, not "interrupting" the pastor "in his preaching," but speaking after his discourse was ended. And had his remarks been acceptable to the people, that is, in harmony with their own opinions, we may be quite sure that no complaint, certainly no appeal to the civil tribunal, would have ensued. It was not his *speaking* during the time of public service, but *what* he said, that was construed, in the heat of an intolerant public sentiment, brooking no departure from the established creed, into a violation of the statute in question. Even the excuse of a grave indiscretion would not be allowed. The law was evidently taken advantage of to make up a case against the apostate, and the judges, Bellingham especially, were more than ready to use it as an instrument of torture. They did not merely pass the judgment they did, because they felt themselves bound by their oath to decide irrespective of their views of the justice or expediency of the law; they cordially approved the statute, and willingly pronounced its penalty.

That these officials were conscientious in so doing, far be it from us to deny; but that cannot relieve them, nor the community which cried out so vehemently for the sacrifice of the distinguished "heretic," of the charge of intolerance. The stern spirit of the theocracy spoke through the law, and through all the proceedings under it, overriding the rights of conscience, and crushing one of the purest and noblest men of the day.

The second trial especially reveals this unhappy spirit, for here there was no alleged interruption of public worship, by open testimony against infant baptism. It was for what he had *not* done, that is, for not presenting his child for baptism, that he was arraigned before the Court. And when, after citing authorities in defence of his conduct, he finally threw himself upon his conscience, "pleading that he could not do it in faith, as all well knew," he was "solemnly admonished of his dangerous error," and bound over under ten pounds sterling to answer at a superior Court. "If," wrote Rev. James Noyes, "a corrupt conscience maketh God's house a den of thieves, *it is meet it should be whipt out.*" Mr. Dunster was presumed to have such a conscience, and it was necessary that it be "whipt out."

In view of the entire proceedings against Mr. Dunster, what can be more appropriate and impressive than his own words,[1] written years before? "I have seen with much shame of face much folly and sin in swelling words and bitter invectives against persons and things where clearness of reason and evidence of God's word is wanting to be matter of conviction to their spirits, against whom such words have been darted."

[1] Page 280.

CHAPTER XII.

IT remains to account, if we can, for the amazement and trepidation with which our Puritan fathers received the advent of a Baptist among them. Thunder in a clear sky, a bomb-shell suddenly bursting over a city in a time of peace, — these may help to represent the consternation awakened by Mr. Dunster's avowal of antipaedobaptism. The entire fabric of Puritandom was shaken to its centre. Church and State took the alarm, and rushed to the rescue.[1]

But how came it to pass that a man, hitherto universally regarded as "learned, conscionable," and pious, should suddenly become an object of general suspicion, dread and persecution? To answer this question, we must understand what were the then prevalent views of the Puritans about infant baptism, anabaptism, and toleration.

[1] See Preface, page 4, note.

These we shall endeavor to exhibit, as a necessary part of the history we are narrating, and, so far as may be, as an apology for the conduct of the Puritan leaders of New England.[1] It will be seen that these men, however mistaken in their views and spirit, yet acted not without reasons satisfactory to their consciences. Like Saul of Tarsus, they verily thought they were doing God service, in persecuting "heretics;" though alas, they did not, like him in his more enlightened years, repent of their wrong.

The great John Cotton shall be our first witness. In his *Grounds and Ends of the Baptism of the Children of the Faithful*, published in 1647, —a work written to answer the scruples which had arisen in the mind of a friend, the son of Pu-

[1] This apology will, of course, apply with equal force to the persecution of Protestants by Roman Catholics. The difference between the two classes is this, that in exercising religious intolerance, the former were inconsistent, the latter in harmony, with the fundamental principles of their respective systems. Persecuting Protestants are for this reason worthy of double blame.

The logical development of Protestantism, whose vital idea is the right of private judgment, has in our day brought unrestricted religious liberty; while Romanism, true to itself, is as intolerant as ever.

ritan parents in England, about the truth of this doctrine, he clearly shows his estimate of infant baptism. It seems that this person's house and goods had been lately consumed by fire, upon which Mr. Cotton remarks: "I fear this hand of God is gone out against you, to visit upon you and your family, your breach of covenant with the Lord and his people" [in withholding his children from baptism]. "For surely," he adds, "it will be your wisest and safest course so to construe God's meaning, that your breach of covenant with God did kindle a fire in his wrath, which brake forth upon your house, and burnt up so great a part of your estate. . . . You saw, not long before, a like fire of God's wrath breaking forth in burning the houses of others of your brethren and neighbors, who had awhile before turned aside into the same way of errors with yourself; which, when you took no meaning by, the same fire burst forth for that last upon yours. How wise and righteous was the hand of the Lord, that when water was neglected to baptize your children, water should be wanting to quench the fire that consumed your house."

"He [Satan] now relinquisheth all those gross

and ungracious tenets whereby he was wont to plead against children's baptism, and now pleadeth no other arguments in these stirring times of reformation than may be urged from a main principle of purity and reformation, to wit : That no duty of God's worship, nor any ordinance of religion is to be administered in the church, but such as hath just warrant from the word of God. And by urging this argument against the baptism of infants, Satan transformeth himself into an angel of light. . . . For if godly parents do withdraw their children from the covenant, and from the seal of the covenant, they do make void (as much as in them lieth) the covenant both to themselves and to their children ; and then will the Lord cut off such souls from his people." [1]

[1] John Spur, in his account of the whipping of Obadiah Holmes in 1651, said : " Mr. Cotton in his sermon immediately before the Court gave their sentence against Mr. Clarke, Obadiah Holmes and John Crandal, affirmed that denying infant baptism would overthrow all, and this was a *capital* offence ; and therefore they were *soul-murderers.* When therefore the Governor, Mr. John Endicott, came into the Court to pass sentence against them, he said thus, *You deserve to die,* but this we agreed upon, that Mr. Clarke shall pay twenty pounds fine, and Obadiah Holmes thirty pounds fine, and John Crandal five pounds, and

To the same effect Thomas Cobbett, pastor at Lynn, in his *Vindication of the Covenant and Church Estate of Children of Church Members*, published in 1643, says: "Ever since that word of old, 'I will put enmity betwixt thee and the woman, and betwixt thy seed and her seed,' Satan hath had a special spite at the seed of the Church. . . . Who seeth not how Satan doth seek by such suggestions to undermine the succession of the true religion, and of true visible churches, which have used to be continued in and by the church seed? . . . How many precious professors, to outward view at least, did at first entertain some scruples about the external interest of church members' children in the covenant and initiatory seal of it, which now peremptorily censure the same as antichristian and human inventions. Let my advice be . . . to take heed of unnecessary discourses and disputes with Satanical suggestions, under what promising and plausible pretences soever they come. . . . It is not the first age or time, that Satanical sugges-

to remain in prison until their fines be either paid or security given for them, or else they are all of them to be well whipped." Backus, I. 194.

tions, '*Thus it is written*,' and '*Thus saith the Lord*,' hath been propounded." "See the danger and detestableness of anabaptistical tenents, giving God and Christ (in part) the lie. . . . And how doth such doctrine undermine all the Churches of the Saints which differ from them?"

In his *Simple Cobbler of Agawam*, Nathaniel Ward, of Ipswich, "lawyer, clergyman and humorist," addresses the Anabaptists: "1. To entreat them to consider what a high pitch of boldness it is for a man to cut a principal ordinance out of the kingdom of God. . . . 2. What a cruelty it is, to divest children of that only external privilege which their Heavenly Father has bequeathed them, to interest them visibly in himself, his Son, his Spirit, his covenant of peace, and the tender bosom of their careful mother the Church. 3. What an inhumanity it is, to deprive parents of that comfort they may take from the baptism of their infants dying in their childhood. 4. How unreasonably and unkindly it is, to interturbe the State and Church with their Amalakitish onsets."

Mr. Mitchell, of Cambridge, whose mind was

so much disturbed by Mr. Dunster's arguments against paedobaptism, was yet so greatly impressed with the importance of the practice, that he "resolved . . . that he would have an argument able to remove a mountain, before he would recede from, or appear against, a truth or practice received among the faithful," — which resolution we cannot wonder at, when we read the following, preserved in Mather's Magnalia:[1] —

"One of his infants dying before it could be brought forth to an orderly baptism, he wrote: 'It was a further sad hand of the Lord that it should dye unbaptized. Though I do not think they are orthodox that hang salvation upon baptism, and not rather upon the covenant, yet, as it appears to be a confirming sign, and as it is an ordinance of grace, so to be deprived of it is a great frown, and a sad intimation of the Lord's anger. And though it may be well with the child notwithstanding (that it becomes me to leave unto the Lord!) yet it is to us a token of displeasure. And what construction of thoughts tending to the Lord's dishonor it may occasion, I know not, that after my labors in public about in-

[1] Book IV.

fant baptism, the Lord should take away my child without and before baptism! Hereby the Lord does again and again make me an example of his displeasure before all men, as if he did say openly, that he hath a special controversy with me, this remarkably taking away one after another. The Lord brings me forth, and makes me go up and down, as one smitten of God: the Lord spits in my face.' "

In a work[1] which appeared after the Synod of 1662, opposition to paedobaptism is thus vigorously described: "We should not choose to put anabaptism as contra-distinct to antichristianism. Take antichrist for all that which is against Christ his mind, Rules, and kingdom, so surely anabaptism is a part of it. Take it for the corruptions of the papacy, how near akin the doctrines and principles of the Papists and Anabaptists are, is showed in a late preface to Mr. Shepard's letter. . . . If to oppose and undermine the kingdom of our Lord Jesus Christ be an antichristian thing, let Scripture, reason and experience speak, whether their [the Anabaptists']

[1] An Answer to the Apologetical Preface &c. By Some of the Elders who were members of the Synod of 1662.

tenets and ways be not highly antichristian. Does not their cutting off so great a part of the subjects of Christ's kingdom as the children of the faithful are (Matt. 19: 14), their changing the frame of the covenant, whereby his visible kingdom in his church is constituted and continued &c., give it (though secretly and under plausible pretences) a most deep and dangerous wound to the interests and progress of Christ's kingdom? And hath not experience shown Anabaptism (with its wonted concomitant errors) to be the vexation and clog of Reformation, ever since the beginning of it?"

Another work[1] published about the same time, pursues a similar line of argument: "The way of the Anabaptists, viz. to admit none to membership and baptism but adult professors — is the straitest way, and one would think it would be a way of great purity, but experience hath abundantly shewed the contrary, that it has been an inlet to great corruption and looseness both in doctrine and practice, and a troublesome, danger-

[1] A Defence of the Answer and Arguments of the Synod met at Boston in the year 1662.

ous underminer of reformation. . . . The Lord hath not set up churches only that a few old Christians may keep one another warm while they live, and then carry away the church into the cold grave with them when they die; but that they might with all care nurse up still another generation of subjects to Christ, that may stand up in his kingdom when they are gone."

In 1672, Urian Oakes, three years afterwards elected President of Harvard College, where he had graduated, in 1649, said in a Discourse: "The fathers took special care for the continuance of the Kingdom of Christ here in after generations, by asserting their [children's] covenant interest therein: and therefore examine the experience of former times, and Anabaptisme we shall find hath ever been lookt at by the Godly Leaders of this people as a Scab to be contended against, being so cruel and hard-hearted an Opinion, an Engine framed to cut the throat of the Infantry of the Church."

Mr. Hubbard,[1] the historian of Massachusetts,

[1] Mr. Hubbard was a graduate of Harvard College, in its first class of 1642, and of course under President Dunster.

said, in a Dedication to an Election Sermon, 1676: "If he were not much mistaken who said it is morally impossible to rivet the Christian religion into the body of a nation without infant baptism, by proportion it will as necessarily follow, that the neglect or disuse thereof will as directly tend to root it out."

To these opinions of eminent ministers, we may add that of a noted man in the government. Mr. Gould[1] (Backus, I. 293), states that one day he met Deputy-Governor Bellingham in Boston, who called to him and said, "'Goodman Gould, I desire you that you would let the church baptize your child;'" and on his saying that he durst not bring out his child (as against his conscience) the Governor "called to Mrs. Norton of Charlestown, and prayed her to fetch Goodman Gould's child and baptize it." It must have been about this time, that Mr. Gould, having been presented by the Grand Jury for denying baptism to his child, was "admonished" by the County Court, (the same Richard Bellingham, then

[1] Mr. Thomas Gould was one of the original members and the first pastor of the first Baptist church of Boston. He had been a member of the Charlestown Congregational Church.

Deputy-governor, being on the bench,) "of his error, and of his greate danger of the Lord's displeasure to himself and perill to his seed, in case he persisted therein, instancing some Scripture examples, as that of Moses, and some other, and gave him some further time to consider of it untill the next County Court at Cambridge.[1] "

Finally, the common estimate of infant baptism was summed up by Increase Mather: "Antipaedobaptism is a blasted error." [2]

Such, then, were the opinions of our Puritan fathers respecting infant baptism. It was, they

[1] Records of Middlesex County Court.

[2] Divine Right of Infant Baptism. It is due to the author of this work to add, that at a later period, in the year 1718, he took part in the ordination of a Baptist (Antipaedobaptist) minister in Boston, and in the Preface to the Ordination Sermon, preached by his son, Cotton, wrote in the following liberal strain: "It was a grateful surprise to me, when several of the brethren of the Antipaedobaptist persuasion came to me, desiring that I would give them the Right Hand of Fellowship in ordaining one whom they had chosen to be their pastor. I did . . . readily consent to what they proposed; considering that . . . all the brethren of the church with whom I have any acquaintance (I hope the like concerning others of them) are, in the judgment of rational charity, godly persons."

contended, indispensable to the very existence of the Church, and of a true Commonwealth.

Their views of toleration were consistent with such views of baptism.

"This is not unfitting," wrote John Cotton in his *Bloody Tenent,* "that a magistrate should draw his sword, though not in matters spirituall, yet *about* matters spirituall to protect them in peace, and to stave off the disturbers and destroyers of them."

"Though spirituall weapons are mighty through God, and sufficient to those ends for which the Lord appointed them ; which are to purge out leaven from their holy communion, and to mortify the flesh of offenders : yet that is not supercedeas to Civill Magistrates to neglect to punish those sins which the Church hath censured, if the persons censured do proceed to subvert the truth of the gospel, or the peace of the Church or the salvation of the people."

"It was toleration that made the Church antichristian ; and the Church never took hurt by the punishment of hereticks."

The Cambridge Platform of 1649, the Book of Discipline for the New England Churches, thus refers to the civil power : —

"Idolatry, Blasphemy, Heresy, venting corrupt and pernicious Opinions that destroy the Foundation, Open Contempt of the Word preached, and the like, are to be restrained and punished by Civill Authority. If any Church, one or more, shall grow Schismaticall, rending itself from the Communion of other Churches, or shall walk incorrigibly or obstinately in any corrupt way of their own, contrary to the Rule of the Word, in such case the Magistrate is to put forth his coercive power, as the matter shall require."

Captain Edward Johnson, a man of note in Massachusetts, in Mr. Dunster's day, wrote as follows, in his *Wonder-Working Providence, &c.*:[1] —

"Familists, Seekers, Antinomians and Anabaptists, they are so ill armed, that they think it best sleeping in a whole skin, fearing that if the day of battell once go on, they shall fall among Antichrist's armies, and therefore cry out like cowards, If you will let me alone, and I will let you alone; but assuredly the Lord Christ hath said, He that is not with us is against us. There is no room in his Army for toleratorists."

[1] Book III. ch. 12.

"To be sure there are many that strive for a Toleration, yet the people of Christ, who are the naturall mothers of this government, resolve never to see their living child so divided."

Addressing the magistrates, he said: "You know right well that the Churches of Christ have not thrived under the tolerating government of Holland, from whence the Lord hath translated one Church already &c."

John Norton, of Boston, declared, that when fundamental errors were openly broached, the "holy tactics of the civil sword should be employed" to suppress them.

The views of Jonathan Mitchell appear from the following extract from an Election sermon, delivered in 1667. Addressing the magistrates, he said: "Do not mar and wrong an excellent work and profession by mixing and weaving in spurious Principles or Practices; as those of Separation, *Anabaptism*, Morellian (anarchical) Confusion, and Licentious *Toleration*. . . . Separation and *Anabaptism* are wonted Intruders and seeming Friends, but secret fatal enemies to Reformation."

Thomas Shepard of Charlestown, a son of

Shepard of Cambridge, said, in his famous Election sermon — "Eye Salve"[1] — in 1672: "It is to be hoped that this coercive power of a godly magistracy, which we have experienced the benefit of so many wayes, being duely managed, shall not be abandoned, nor therefore a repealing of any wholesome law about religion for the defence and maintenance of the gospel among us; or that liberty should be proclaimed to men of any religion to come and set up Shops or Schools of Seduction among us." "'Tis Satan's policy to plead for an indefinite and boundless toleration."

"I look," said Urian Oakes, in 1672, "upon an unbounded Toleration as the first-born of all Abominations. If this should be once born and brought forth among us, you may call it Gad, and give the same reason that *she* did of the name of her son: *Behold, a troop cometh,* even a troop of all manner of Abominations. . . . No doubt but it belongs to the Magistrate to judge what is tolerable in his dominions in this respect. And the eye of the civil magistrate is to be to the securing of the way of God that is duly established. . . . Boundless liberty will expose us to great

[1] Artillery Election Sermon.

danger." The next year,[1] Mr. Oakes was of the same mind, only, if possible, a little more vehement: "Wanton Gospellers, giddy Professors, men of corrupt mindes, would have magistrates that will allow them in publishing and spreading their damnable Heresies, disturbing the Peace and Order of the Churches of Christ, and spurning all that is precious and sacred amongst us."

In 1674, Mr. Arnold, of Marshfield, in an Election sermon, advocated the same doctrine: "Tolerate not things that are intolerable. A boundless Toleration will be found at last an intolerable thing. Such as differ only in Circumstantials, controversial points, and are quiet, peaceable, moderate, and do not busy themselves in learning others, we may and must bear with them; but when persons err in Fundamentals, deny Christ Jesus, the Word of God, Eternal Election &c., such Heresies and Hereticks must be suppressed."

Indeed it was commonly said in Massachusetts, that "Antichrist was coming in at the back-door, by a general liberty of conscience."

Governor Hutchinson told the truth when he

[1] New England Pleaded With, an Election Sermon.

said: "Toleration was preached against [in New England] as a sin in rulers, which would bring down the judgments of heaven upon the land."

The time had not yet come for the utterance, by a New England Puritan minister, of such sentiments as the following, contained in a sermon by Thomas Prince, of Boston, in the year 1731–2: "How opposite to Christian charity and union is it, for the imposers [of things which they own Christ has not appointed] to make themselves judges of the hearts of those who differ from them, and engross the sacred name of Conscience to themselves, by asserting the dissent of others is from humor only, and not from conscience." "And how exceeding beautiful would be the Christian world . . . where they differ about an ordinance of his [Christ's], these both preserve their brethren's consciences entire, and believe in charity they differ from a conscientious regard to what they apprehend to be Christ's appointment."

Had this simple gospel rule been in vogue from the first in New England, some dark and disagreeable shadows which now rest upon her early history, had happily been wanting. But the Puritans, believing, as they did, that the unrestricted expression of religious opinions would be "damageful," if not ruinous, to church and state, proceeded, with stern consistency, to carry out their principles of intolerance into practice. Laws were enacted to defend that form of faith and worship which they themselves had accepted as the genuine gospel, and to suppress whatever, and punish whomsoever, differed from or was opposed to it. And as Anabaptism (as they insisted on calling the system of the Baptists) was in their view a concentration of heresies, a *monstrum horrendum*, aiming a deadly thrust at the church, through its rejection of infant baptism, it very early received particular attentions from the managers of the Theocracy. "Experience tells us," wrote Samuel Willard, of Boston, "that such a rough thing as a New England Baptist is not to be handled over tenderly." Ministers and civilians of an earlier day were precisely of his mind, as the Statute Book of Massachusetts abundantly proves. Thus, in 1644, it was enacted by the General Court, that "if any Christian shall openly condemn the baptizing of infants, or shall purposely depart the congregation at the administration of that ordinance, . . . continuing obstinate therein, he shall be sentenced to be banished."

Anabaptists still increasing, a more elaborate law was passed "for banishing," as Winthrop has it, "such as continued obstinate after due conviction." It was as follows: "Forasmuch as experience hath plentifully and often proved, that since the first rising of the Anabaptists, about one hundred years since, they have been the incendiaries of commonwealths, and the infectors of persons in main matters of religion, and the troublers of churches in all places where they have been, and that they *who have held the baptizing of infants unlawful, have usually held other errors or heresies together therewith,* though they have (as other heretics use to do) *concealed the same* till they spied out a fit advantage and opportunity to vent them, by way of question or scruple; and whereas divers of this kind have since our coming into New England appeared amongst ourselves, some whereof (as others before them) denied the ordinance of magistracy, and the lawfulness of making war, and others the lawfulness of magistrates, and their inspection into any breach of the first table; which opinions, if they should be connived at by us, are like to be increased amongst us, so must necessarily bring guilt upon us, infection and trouble to the churches, and hazard to the whole commonwealth ; it is ordered and agreed, that if any person or persons, within this jurisdiction, shall either *openly condemn or oppose the baptizing of infants*, or go about secretly to seduce others from the approbation or use thereof, or shall purposely depart the congregation at the ministration of the ordinance, or shall deny the ordinance of magistracy, or their lawful right and authority to make war, or to punish the outward breaches of the first table, and shall appear to the Court wilfully and obstinately to continue therein after due time and means of conviction, every such person or persons shall be *sentenced to banishment*." [1]

The law was not a dead letter. That very year, a man for refusing to suffer his child to be baptized, was tied up and whipped. Winthrop says he suffered "for reproaching the Lord's ordinance." This poor man was not of consequence enough to be banished; he was only whipped!

[1] Col. Rec. II. 85.

The next year after the above law was passed, "upon a petition of divers persons for consideration of the law against Anabaptists, the Court voted, that the law mentioned should not be altered at all, nor explained."[1]

The year following, the Court record reads thus: "The petition [of 78 persons in Dorchester and Roxbury] for the continuance, without abrogation or *weakening*, of the orders in force against Anabaptists and other erroneous persons, is granted."[2]

In 1646, a law was passed, for punishing contemptuous behavior towards God's word and messengers.[3]

The enforcement in 1651, of the law of 1644

[1] Col. Records, II. 141.

[2] Ib. II. 149.

[3] Page 132. It was with reference to this law that Edward Winslow wrote in 1646: "Against Anabaptists, it is true, we have a severe law, but we never did or will execute the rigor of it upon any, and have men living amongst us, nay, some in our churches, of that judgment; and as long as they carry themselves peacefully, as hitherto they do, we will leave them to God, ourselves having performed the duty of brethren to them." Hypocrisy Unmasked, p. 101. The strangers from Rhode Island, and later, President Dunster, had another story to tell.

upon several Baptists has already been referred to.[1] And now Mr. Dunster is passing under the Puritan rod. He had put himself among "the incendiaries of commonwealths," "the infectors of persons in main matters of religion" and "the troublers of churches;" and though as yet he had departed from the Puritan faith at only this single point of baptism, being, for aught they knew to the contrary, as sound as the soundest in the cardinal doctrines of the gospel, yet, as "they who hold the baptizing of infants to be unlawful, usually hold other errors or heresies therewith, though *concealing* the same till they have spied out a fit opportunity to vent them," he was regarded as holding in embryo all possible opinions subversive of the truth. He had started upon a road which was antichristian, and of course tending downward. Besides, the Puritan fathers believed that anabaptism, or antipaedobaptism, was an emanation from the Father of lies.[2] The "scruples and thoughts" against in-

[1] Page 111.

[2] At a later period, Cotton Mather took a more catholic view: "Infant baptism hath been scrupled by multitudes in our day, who have been in other points most worthy Christians, and as

fant baptism which were "injected" into Mr. Mitchell's mind as the result of his conversation with Mr. Dunster, were "from the EVIL ONE." Poor Mr. Dunster was not, then, simply a heretic, misled by his perverted reason; he was in league with Satan, or, at least, was instigated and used by the Prince of Darkness to "undermine" the "true churches." The Cambridge pastor clearly saw this, and luckily escaped the snare into which his once beloved teacher had fallen. And now Satan must be foiled; and the more eminent the instrument of his "devices," the more necessary that he be stripped of his influence. Mr. Dunster, misguided, wretched man, would not see his errors, would "stand by them" and "dare not deny" them, and he must be put where he cannot corrupt the "hope of the flock."

To our minds, looking back from our more enlightened and liberal age, which enjoys the light of all past experience, the comic and the tragic seem strangely blended in the events connected with Mr. Dunster's "martyrdom." Who can but smile, if he do not laugh outright, at the parox-

holy, watchful, fruitful and heavenly people as perhaps any in the world." Magnalia, Bk. VII. 27.

ysms of pious terror which seized upon our Puritan sires because of an *opinion*, a harmless one at that, and at their grave suspicions of good, honest, praying Mr. Dunster as laboring under a demoniacal possession? There is something exceedingly ludicrous in the whole affair; we should also say contemptible, were it not that some of the best and most sensible men that ever lived were concerned in it.

Tantæne animis cœlestibus iræ?

But let us learn a lesson of humility and charity. We laugh at the absurdities of the generations which preceded us, and in our turn we may be found vulnerable to the shafts of ridicule. Still, we are not therefore to gloss over the follies and errors of the past, but to study them in a philosophic, Christian spirit, and make them helps to our own wiser and better living.

CHAPTER XIII.

TO return to our narrative. It will be recollected that on the 24th of October, 1654, Mr. Dunster had resigned; that on the 4th of November he had sent a Petition to the General Court, which was replied to adversely; that on the 10th of November he had addressed to the Court "Considerations" showing why he should not be at once removed from the President's house; that permission was granted him to remain till March, 1655; and that after the expiration of this time, on the 3d of April, a presentment was made against him by the Grand Jury to the County Court, at Cambridge, for "contemptuous treatment of God's word and messengers," for which he was sentenced to receive a public admonition on Lecture day, and to give bonds for good behavior, — to which sentence he responded by letter the following day.[1]

[1] Page 132.

His situation was now very uncomfortable, driven as he was from the College, from his home, and the victim of a civil prosecution: and this may have moved the Corporation and Overseers, in the "Brief Information of the present necessities of the College," which they presented to the General Court, on the 9th of May, 1655, "with earnest desires of their speedy and effectual help for supply," to make the following suggestions about Mr. Dunster: "First. We are indebted to Mr. Dunster, as expended upon account, near £40, notwithstanding that he hath all that we have been able to pay or assign him. Justice and equity requires that this be paid him, being due debt, and apparent upon diligent examination of accounts. Also, besides what is due upon a strict account, that former motion sometime made by a former committee of a hundred pounds to be allowed Mr. Dunster in consideration of his extraordinary pains in raising up and carrying on the College for so many years past. We desire it may be seriously considered, and hope it may make much for *the country's honorable discharge* in the hearts of all, and perpetual encouragement of their servants in such public works, if it be attended."

Of course it was only an act of honesty, especially as more than six months had now expired since Mr. Dunster's resignation, that what was due him from the College should be paid, and it required no great magnanimity in the Board to say so. But it is pleasant to find that they went further, and ventured, with honorable importunity, in the face of the bluff repulse[1] given by the magistrates to Mr. Dunster's petition for "allowance . . . for *extraordinary* labors," to recommend to that same body a generous recognition of his "*extraordinary* pains."

The magistrates, Endicott being now Governor, referred this, with other matters mentioned in the "Information," to the Deputies, as requiring "serious agitation and speedy action," but gave no further hint of their wishes. Evidently the "extraordinary pains" of the ex-president for fourteen years, awakened no grateful sympathy among them. A cold reference without a recommendation. The Deputies took up the case, and found it "meet . . . to satisfy Mr. Dunster what shall be *truly due him on account.*" "The result of the whole affair was," says Quincy, "that he

[1] Pages 149, 150.

obtained nothing from the General Court; and that the Corporation, *after his death,* paid to his widow twenty pounds, in full of the balance due to his estate." Not only did the Court refuse to recognize any "extraordinary" service performed by Mr. Dunster; they delayed paying what they confessed to be his due, for more than five years. Such was the sort of "encouragement" given to the country's "servants." Yet, says Quincy, speaking of the first two Presidents, "for learning, talent and fidelity" they have been "surpassed by no one of their successors;" they "exceeded every one of them in sufferings, sacrifices and privations; . . . they were both main supports of the institution for thirty years, and were not inferior to any of its friends, patrons, or officers, in establishing its character and perpetuating its usefulness."

From this time we hear no more of Mr. Dunster in any transaction with the College, though we know that he retained his affection for it to the last, as appears from his dying wish to be buried in Cambridge.

CHAPTER XIV.

BUT now, while his brethren are alienated from him, and Church and State are arrayed against him, he must seek a home beyond the limits of Massachusetts. Here they will not permit him to teach, or preach, or exercise any other "liberal" profession. Fortunately the Pilgrim Colony is more tolerant than its sister of the Bay, and thither, as Roger Williams had done before him, he will direct his steps.[1]

[1] It is interesting to contrast the persecuting spirit which ruled in Massachusetts with the more catholic tone of the Plymouth government. We have seen with what severity the Baptists were treated in the former Colony — such as Roger Williams, Lady Moody, Clarke, Holmes, and Crandal, and President Dunster. But when Holmes and others were presented to the General Court at Plymouth, they were "only charged to desist from their practice," and "no sentence appears upon record against them." (Backus, I. 177.) The severest punishment inflicted upon the Baptist Church at Rehoboth, founded in 1663 by Rev. John Miles (the first Baptist Church in what is now

But meanwhile we find him in Charlestown, in September, 1655, at the house of Thomas Gould,[1] now also a sufferer, as he is afterwards to be to a far greater extent, for the same cause which had driven Dunster from the College. This person, who, in 1665, became pastor of a Baptist church, now the First Baptist church of Boston, was then under the discipline of the Charlestown church, for refusing to bring his child to baptism, having, it is supposed, been led by Mr. Dunster's discourses on baptism, to renounce his former views about that ordinance.[2] The occasion which called Mr. Dunster to his house was a meeting of thanksgiving held there for some domestic "mercy," to which Mr. Gould had invited a number of his friends. It so happened that during the meeting a letter came to Mr. Gould from the elders of the church, desiring his attendance the next day at "the elder's house"

Massachusetts), was to order the removal of "their meeting into some other place, where they may not prejudice any other church," and to assign them for that purpose "an ample grant" of what was afterwards called Swanzea, where "they made a regular settlement," and lived in peace. (Backus, I. 285.)

[1] Backus, I. 290. [2] Backus.

for a conference upon his case. The letter was shown among others, to Mr. Dunster, who advised Gould to comply with their request.

It is noteworthy, that Mr. Dunster is mentioned by Mr. Gould, in his account of the affair, as among his "friends;" and it certainly speaks much for the ex-president's humility, strength of character, and regard for his principles, that he should permit himself to be thus identified with a plain man, who, also, though acknowledged to be "of a grave and serious spirit, and of sober conversation,"[1] was laboring under church discipline and reproach. But under present circumstances, the sympathy and friendship of the humblest person, especially if a fellow-sufferer for conscience' sake, must have been very grateful to Mr. Dunster's feelings, deserted and persecuted as he was by those who occupied the higher positions in the community, his former associates and brethren. It seems not unlikely that, had he been living at the time, he might have been found united with Mr. Gould and nine others, in 1665, in establishing a Baptist church. But the hour had not yet come for such a move-

[1] Hubbard, History of New England.

ment, and Mr. Dunster was led by Providence into another field, where he died before a Baptist church was formed in either the Massachusetts or Plymouth Colony.

The town of Scituate in the latter colony, which comprised all the present territory of the counties of Plymouth, Barnstable and Bristol, except Hingham, is only twenty-eight miles from Boston, just across the line which separated the two provinces; but it was far enough to be beyond the jurisdiction of the General Court of the Puritans, and could therefore afford a shelter and a field of usefulness to the exile from Massachusetts.

Deane, in his History of Scituate, says that Mr. Dunster removed to that place "immediately after his resignation," where, he adds, "we find notices of him the same autumn employed in the ministry, in which he continued nearly five years." [1]

[1] Backus (I. 453) says: "By searching into these matters, Mr. Dunster . . . was brought openly to renounce infant baptism; and seeing the temper that was discovered in the Massachusetts, he removed into Plymouth Colony, the very year that Reyner moved out of it," which was Nov. 1654.

Among all the towns of the more tolerant Plymouth, Scituate deserves honorable mention for its friendly treatment of dissenters. It had also peculiar attractions for a person of Baptist tendencies. In the year 1634, Rev. John Lothrop, an Independent minister, and the company which came with him from Kent, in England, settled in Scituate and established a church. The church to which they had belonged in the mother country had been divided on the subject of baptism, a portion seceding, in 1633, to establish a Baptist church under Mr. Jesse. "Those," says Deane, "who came with" Mr. Lothrop, "seem not all to have been fully settled on this point, and they found others in Scituate ready to sympathize with them." The controversy of previous years followed them to America, and "divided them again," which "appears from the fact, that many of those who remained at Scituate after his [Mr. Lothrop's] removal to Barnstable, brought in Mr. Chauncy for their pastor, ... and eagerly adopted his mode of immersion." During Mr. Chauncy's pastorate, "there seemed to be three parties in Scituate, one of which held to infant sprinkling, another to adult immersion exclusively, and a third to immersion of infants as well as adults," Mr. Chauncy belonging to the last.

The advent therefore of even the most malignant Baptist would strike no such terror into the minds of the people of Scituate, as had the announcement of Mr. Dunster's anabaptism, among the people of Massachusetts. They were quite familiar with this delusion of Satan! And so he was doubtless welcomed as a learned and able minister; and, in spite of his antipaedobaptist views, he appears to have served the church in Scituate for several years, though not probably in the capacity of pastor.[1] Persecution would likely have forced him to a clear separation from the established churches, but as it was, he probably never identified himself with a Baptist church, as indeed in his lifetime there was scarcely an opportunity of doing. We judge that he was content, under the circumstances, to remain in fellowship with his Independent brethren so long as they did not interfere with his liberty of

[1] Deane says it is not known whether he was "regularly inducted into office." Baylies says that "he occasionally preached," which seems the more probable.

conscience. It is greatly to the credit of the people of Scituate, that the true doctrine of the rights of conscience had made such progress among them ; as also appears from their subsequent mild treatment of the Quakers.

There must have been at this time much excellent society in Scituate. " Many of the fathers [of the town] were men of good education and easy fortune, who had left homes altogether enviable, save in the single circumstance of the abridgment of their religious liberty. In 1639, this town contained more men of distinguished talents and fair fortune than it has at any period since. They were 'the men of Kent,' celebrated in English history as men of gallantry, loyalty and courtly manners. Gilson, Vassall, Hatherly, Cudworth, Tilden, Hoar, Foster, Stedman, Saffin, Hinckley, and others had been accustomed to the elegancies of life of England."[1] Some of these, we know, were living when Mr. Dunster removed to Scituate, and among them were three persons whom he must have found congenial spirits, Hatherly, Cudworth and Robinson. The first had been a London merchant, and was now

[1] Deane, page 151.

a large landowner in the Colony, and a man of great worth and influence. He was a prominent member of the church, and had been a special friend and admirer of Mr. Chauncy; and in a civil capacity, he had not only distinguished himself for many years, in the various positions of Assistant, Treasurer of the Colony, and Commissioner of the United Colonies, but by what is far higher, as it was then a rarer quality, a tolerant spirit toward persons of a different faith. Captain, afterwards General James Cudworth, a particular friend of Hatherly, and who had accompanied him from England in 1632, at different times held important offices in the civil administration, as Assistant, Deputy, Commissioner and Deputy Governor. Isaac Robinson, a son of the great John Robinson, "the father of independency," was at one time Assistant in the Government. When, after 1657, the persecution began against the Quakers, as well as against those who harbored them or favored their sentiments, these three men took a resolute stand against these oppressive measures, for which, in consequence, they fell under the displeasure of the majority in the councils of the Colony, being, with some others who sympathized with them, left out of office and disfranchised. Captain Cudworth was most conspicuous in this opposition to the persecuting policy. As one of the Commissioners of the United Colonies, he refused, in 1657, to sign the document which that body addressed to the government of Rhode Island, recommending "that means be taken to banish the Quakers," and from this time he himself became an object of persecution. When, two years later, he was returned as Deputy from Scituate, the Court refused him a seat. A letter which, about this time, he wrote to England, made him specially obnoxious to the government, but it remains as a noble monument to his generous character. Its spirit will appear from the following passage: —

"As to the state and condition of things amongst us, it is sad, and so like to continue. The antichristian, persecuting spirit is very active, and that in the powers of this world. He that will not lash, persecute and punish men that differ in matters of religion, must not sit on the bench, nor sustain any office in the Commonwealth. Last election, Mr. Hatherly and myself were left off the bench, and myself discharged of my captainship, because I had entertained some of the Quakers at my house, thereby that I might be the better acquainted with their principles. I thought it better to do so, than with the blind world to censure, condemn, rail at, and revile them, when they neither saw their persons nor knew any of their principles. But the Quakers and I cannot close in divers things, and so I signified to the Court; but told them withal, that as I was no Quaker, so I would be no persecutor."

Men who were capable of expressing and acting out such admirable sentiments, the like of which were not elsewhere heard from Pilgrim or Puritan, could not fail to sympathize with the persecuted exile from Massachusetts. Mr. Dunster had probably been acquainted with their character before this time, as he must have been with their names and social position, though the Quaker persecution had not yet made specially conspicuous their catholic views. Doubtless they took him by the hand, and their large hearts gave him a hearty welcome to their town and their homes. The affection and esteem which Mr. Cudworth had for him appears in the letter referred to above, written some four years after

Mr. Dunster's removal to Scituate: "Through mercy we have yet among us the worthy Mr. Dunster, whom the Lord hath made boldly to bear testimony against the spirit of persecution," — a notice honorable alike to both. This incidental allusion to Mr. Dunster, only the year before his death, is a gratifying testimony to his consistent devotion to the last, to the principles which he had avowed, and for which he had suffered in Massachusetts. Morton,[1] speaking of Mr. Dunster in Scituate, says that he "was useful in helping to oppose their [the Quakers'] abominable opinions, and in defending the truth against them;" but in this he did no more than Roger Williams, who had a sharp controversy with George Fox, but refused to persecute him or his adherents. Mr. Dunster opposed their views, but defended their persons. He could not so far forget how himself had suffered for his opinions, as to act the part of a persecutor. On the other hand, "the Lord" "made" him "boldly to bear testimony against the spirit of persecution."

In 1656, Mr. Dunster's peace was somewhat

[1] Memorials, 283.

disturbed by a suit instituted against him in the County Court, at Cambridge, by his step-son, John Glover,[1] for the recovery of property, such as "houses, lands, goods, debts, &c.," in the possession of Mr. Dunster, and alleged to belong to the plaintiff by the will of his father, or of Elisabeth, his wife, whom Mr. Dunster had married, in 1641. At this late day, and from the imperfect records which remain, it is impossible to accurately determine the real merits of the case; but it appears probable that the decision of the Bench of Magistrates, to whom, by mutual agreement, the matter was at length referred, by which Mr. Glover's claim was reduced from £1,447 &c. to £117 &c. "leaving some debts . . . to the value

[1] He was a physician, and removed to England. In a letter (Hist. Col. "Dunster Papers") from William Cutler to Mr. Dunster, under date of May 19, 1654, the writer says: "Your sonne Mr. Jno. Glover cald att our house as he went into Scotland to be over the hospitale with Coll. fenwicks brother: *I hope he will prove honest.*" It will perhaps be unfair to interpret this expression unfavorably to Mr. Glover. May it not mean, I hope he will do well — prove himself a man? The word "honest," at that time, expressed the idea of *honorable*, *becoming*, as in the translation of Rom. xii. 17. *Provide things honest in the sight of all men*, i.e. so conduct as to gain the good opinion of men.

of £57 11*s*. 6 pence, to be further cleared by the said Henry &c.," was accepted as a final adjustment.

It is easy to see that some difference of opinion might arise as to the expenses incident to the maintenance and education of several children during a guardianship of many years; but the reputation for integrity which Mr. Dunster universally enjoyed during his lifetime, and the profound respect with which even his most inveterate opposers spoke of him after his decease, forbid us to doubt that he acted the part of a conscientious and judicious guardian. Several years before, he had petitioned the General Court to appoint a Committee "to view and examine what the estates of Roger and John Glover are, in the hands of the said Dunster &c." In his Petition to the Court, the next month after his resignation,[1] he thus referred to the action of that body upon his request:

"Whereas this honored Court the 3d of this present month voted a Committee to examine all accounts of your petitioner in reference to the estate of Mr. Jon Glover or what his last wife

[1] Page 145.

left, or which may concern the estate contended for, &c., your petitioner humbly conceiveth, prayeth and hopeth that you will readily reverse that vote as requiring an impossibility at our hand; for how should your petitioner, unlesse a Joseph or a Daniel, give an account of a Gentleman's Estate dead above 16 years agoe, whom nor whose estate he never knew, neither ever was Legatee immediately, Executor, Administrator or Assignee? nay who may justly say, that he never knew any estate was in law his, seeing there was noe Inventory at all annexed to his Will though legally proved. Neither did the last deceased wife of your petitioner leave any Estate (after debts discharged contracted in her life time) in this country save the lands at Cambridge with the buildings thereon, and a farme at Sudbury, the title whereof your honor's Court according to the Record must determine ere that your petitioner can give any account thereof. And as for what may concern the estate contended for by the 2 sonnes or any other, &c., your petitioner desireth humbly to be excused from such an infinite task, who yet is willing to give a faithfull and fatherly account and make satisfaction to the full content of the 2 children of the aforesaid Mr. Glover, that have not fully received their child's portion, viz. Mr. John Glover and Mrs. Priscilla Appleton, and to answer all sutes and pleas that any other of the children shall for any Estate in this country legally make, during your humble petitioner's life. Otherwise it is easily foreseen what endlesse vexations and tedious decisions both this honored Court, your humble petitioner and his posterity, may from generation to generation causelessly be put to."

The Court, as we have shown, having treated the other requests of Mr. Dunster in a "heartless" manner, contrary to the plainest requirements of equity and humanity, were equally indisposed to make any concession in the present case. Their spirit was inexorable, they persisted in demanding the pound of flesh, evidently with the purpose of bringing every thing to bear upon the one object before them — crushing the heretic, and driving him out of the Colony.

CHAPTER XV.

THE persecutions of Mr. Dunster seem to have awakened a deep interest among the Baptists of the mother country, and on the 10th of July, 1656, he received a letter from a leading member of that denomination in Dublin, Ireland, expressing the sympathy of his brethren there, in the trials he had experienced, and urging him to make that place his future home :

" Ffor his truely Esteemed ffreind Mr Dunstor : late Provost of the Colleage at Cambridge in New England,

these

Honored Freind,

I am wholly a stranger to you further then as to Report which hath spread it selfe to ye rejoicing of many y^t feare ye Lord, and hearing that your Porcon hath been to suffer in some measure for ye Crosse of Christ, my selfe and some other that truly Love you on ye ground aforesaid made it our Request to ye truly vertuous Lord Deputy to provide for you in this Land, who readily Embraced the same, and ordered fifty pound for ye bringing over yourselfe and family, as you may see by a Copy of his Lorpps [Lordship's] and Councells inclosed, with Direccons for mee to send to you, which moneys I have sent by Mr. John Milam of Waterford, once an Inhabitant of New England, and who will send to you and Contrive yor passadg, and advise you as to ye state of this Countrey and ye Christians amongst us. You need not feare Accomodacons here, though I hope that will not be your cheife motive, but rather hono^r^ of ye Lord and his great name. You may through mercy have free liberty of your Conscience ; and opportunity of Assotiateing with Saints and free publishing ye Ghospell of Truth, which [is] greatly wanted amongst us, there being but few able and painefull men who make ye service of God theire sake. I pray be not discouraged att any thing you have heard or shall heare of this place,[1] but consider ye Prov-

1 "As to the grand affairs in Ireland, especially as it relates to the Anabaptist party, I am confident that they are much mis-

idence of God who soe unexpectedly as to you calls for your remove. Paul did not in like case conferr with ffesh and blood (hapily you may have Lesse reason in some respect soe to doe). I desire you to have a Care, knoweing that there is a Crafty one that lyes in waite for to deceive. I shall Add noe more but desire you to Consider that it is ye duty of a Christian to be guided by ye Call of God, and to be and doe whatever he shall require from you, by which Rule I desire you to walke, and the God of mercy be your Councello^r^ herein, and guide you in the way he would have you to walke, and that his presence may attend you to the perfecting your Race with Joy, and witnessing a good Confession before men, that soe in ye end you may be perfected in the Joy and Glory of the Lord att his appearance. In whome I trust to be found.

Yours and all Saints sincere freind and Servt,

EDW. ROBERTS.[1]

conceived in England. Truly I am apt to believe, that upon the change of affairs here was discontent, but very little animosity." State Papers, II. 149. Let. of Edw. Roberts to Secretary Thurloe, April 5, 1654.

[1] Mr. Roberts was a Welshman, who, with several others of

Dublin 3[d] 1655."

[Labelled, "Received, 10th of July, 1656, from y[e] hand of goodwife Price, y[e] order of y[e] consel inclosed."][1]

The "free liberty of conscience" enjoyed under Cromwell's administration, in the mother country, is notably in contrast with the intolerance practised at the same time in the Massachusetts dependency. The Puritans of New England had not kept pace with the Puritans of Old England. Owen was in advance of Cotton, and Sir Richard Saltonstall,[2] writing from

the same religious persuasion, settled in Ireland. In 1683, an Epistle was sent by Irish Baptists, of ten different churches, to their brethren in London, recommending a day of fasting, and a correspondence among all the Baptist churches of England, Scotland, Wales and Ireland. Among the signers from the church in Dublin we find the name of Edward Roberts. Ivimey. Hist. of English Baptists.

1 Hist. Col. IV. ser. I. 251.

2 He was called by Mather that "excellent knight," and by Johnson, that "much honored and upright-hearted servant of Christ." In his letter he said, "First, you compel such to come into your assemblies as you know will not join you in your worship; and when they show their dislike thereof, or witness against it, then you stir up your magistrates to punish them for such (as you conceive) their public affronts. . . . These rigid ways have laid you very low in the hearts of the saints."

England, in 1652, had felt constrained to rebuke the "tyranny and persecutions of New England," in the case of the Rhode Island visitors at Lynn. Later, in 1669, on the occasion of the further persecution of the Baptists in Boston, thirteen Puritan divines of England, including Dr. Goodwin and Dr. Owen, addressed a letter to Governor Bellingham, advising that "an end" be put "unto the sufferings and confinements of the persons censured, and to restore them to their former liberty." [1]

Henry Cromwell, a younger son of the Protector, and, at the time of Mr. Roberts' writing, Lord Deputy of Ireland, was a man of eminently catholic spirit. Thurloe,[2] Secretary to Oliver

[1] As late as 1719–20, Dr. Isaac Watts, in a letter to Cotton Mather, referring to Neal's exposure, in his History of New England, of "the persecuting principles and practices of the first planters," said: "But methinks it would be better to have such cruel and sanguinary statutes as those under the title of heresy, repealed in form, and by the public authority of the nation, and if the appearance of this book [Neal's History] in your country shall awaken your General Assembly to attempt and fulfil such a noble piece of service to your country, there will be a happy effect of that part of the history which now *makes us blush and ashamed.*" Mass. Hist. Col. I. series, V. 200.

[2] State Papers, VII. 454.

and Richard Cromwell, bears honorable testimony to this fact, when he says: "Henry Cromwell . . . discovered his enlightened liberality and correct views of religious freedom equally with the most distinguished persons of the age. He was a genuine lover and firm promoter of unrestricted religious emancipation, by openly rejecting all impositions in religion." In the same strain is Henry Cromwell's own letter to Fleetwood, in which he says: "Dear Brother, let us not fall into the sins of other men, lest we partake of their plagues. Let it be so carried, that all the people of God, though under different forms, yea, even those whom you count without, may enjoy their birthright and civil liberty, and that no one party may tread upon the neck of another. What have these done, that their blood should be the price of our lust and ambition?"

It is no wonder that such a man, when made acquainted with Mr. Dunster's persecutions, should be deeply interested in him, and zealously second the plan for his removal.

And it must have been peculiarly grateful to Mr. Dunster's feelings to find his course meeting with such warm approval and sympathy even among strangers. For reasons which we may readily conjecture, he saw fit to decline the above generous invitation, though we cannot doubt that he responded with deep emotion. He had long before chosen New England for his home, and here he wished to live and die. Here his affections had taken root, and doubtless it would have cost him many a pang to tear himself from the beloved soil. We must also believe, that even at this time, the thought was to him a pleasant one, that Cambridge, dear, though so ungrateful, should be his final resting-place. Besides, he was no longer in persecuting Massachusetts. Scituate had given him a kindly welcome within the precincts of the Pilgrims, and here he had doubtless formed strong and tender attachments. We are glad he did not go. His grave is with us to this day, and is also where it best should be, amid the very scene of his arduous labors in the cause of learning, and of his nobler sufferings in behalf of what he believed to be God's truth.

CHAPTER XVI.

MR. DUNSTER died at Scituate, Feb. 27, 1659, nearly five years after his resignation at Cambridge. The year before (1658), he had made his will, which, with characteristic piety, began as follows:[1] "O Lord, my times are in thy hands, and I fully submitt unto thine appoyntments for my dissolution, committinge my spirit into thy hands, for thou hast redeemed it, and hast, by manifold deliverances out of Tribulation, sealed to my soule the truth of thy word concerninge thy fatherly love and care of me, but especially by thine own secret and cleare spirit of grace sealing to my heart that which no mortall understanding or spirit could possibly conceive without God," &c. In the will, he provided for his burial at Cambridge, directing that "twenty shillings be allowed to any that shall transport

[1] See page 303.

my body to Charlestowne, or if to Cambridge, thirty shillings, and five shillings apiece to eight bearers that shall carry it from Charlestowne to Cambridge there to be enterred by my loveing wife and other relaccons." He appointed President Chauncy and Mr. Mitchell, "his reverend and trusty friends and brethren," to appraise his library, and bequeathed them several books, which were specified; and it is with particular reference to this part of the will, that Quincy well says: "Dunster possessed a gentle heart, and a noble vein of Christian charity." Mr. Chauncy "had taken his place at the College," and Mr. Mitchell was the one who, five years before, had been "fearful to go needlessly to Mr. Dunster," because he "found a venom and a poison in his insinuations and discourses against Paedobaptism," thinking that "they were from the EVIL ONE."

Indeed "the injury [he received at Cambridge] seems to have cut too deeply for resentment; but his yearning in death after the beloved spot where he had so faithfully labored, gives touching evidence how keenly he must have felt it."[1]

The spirit which led him to direct that his

[1] Letter in New York Examiner, by Mrs. H. C. Conant.

body should be taken to Cambridge for interment, finds its explanation, in part, we think, in what he had said in his "Considerations" addressed, in 1654, to the General Court: "The whole transaction of this business is such which *in process of time, when all things come to mature consideration*, may very probably *create grief* on all sides; *yours subsequent*, as mine antecedent. I am not the man you take me to be." Conscious of having acted in the fear of God, he believed that time and reflection would change the feelings of hostility which had driven him from the College, into a just appreciation of his motives. And presuming, doubtless, that such a change had already begun, as appears especially from his brotherly mention of Mr. Mitchell in his will, he wishes to be laid to rest in Cambridge. He may have thought that the sight of his dead body would help to soften whatever asperity remained, and to give him again that place in the consideration of the good people of Massachusetts which he felt had never been withheld through any fault of his own. He ought to have lived and died in Cambridge, — this he would say by his interment there. It would be taking him back to his old home. Yet it would also show that he cherished no resentment. He would be buried among his former friends, between whom and himself a sorrowful shadow had been cast — but only a shadow.

This loving and forgiving spirit towards those who had so deeply wronged him shed a beautiful radiance over the last days of Mr. Dunster. He was proved to be thoroughly good as well as great — a man to be loved even more than to be admired. All his great services in the cause of sacred and liberal learning while at Cambridge, were cast quite into the shade by the Christlike charity and humility which characterized his obscurity at Scituate, and especially his farewell to the world.

Morton says that "his body was embalmed, and removed to Cambridge, and there honorably buried;" as Hubbard says, "solemnly interred." We are glad to know this. At the burial-scene, past differences were doubtless forgotten, or viewed in a milder light. Many, we would fain believe, who had honored and loved him in other years, before the unhappy breach, now shed tears of sincere grief — such "grief" as Mr. Dunster had predicted, — as they gathered about the grave. After all — so they must have thought then, for they had kind Christian hearts — after all that we once said and did to his injury, he was a good man, and did a noble work — we judged him too hastily and harshly. Mitchell, the Cambridge pastor, must have been prominent on the occasion, and have spoken kind words of his former teacher and friend. He could no longer think of him as an emissary of the Evil One. When he went from the grave, he composed an elegy, as "a respectful tribute to his memory."

We would like to know that Bellingham, then Deputy Governor, was there, to make some atonement by his presence at the funeral of the dead saint, for his harsh treatment, as Governor, of the living President. But, whoever were there, all hearts must have been subdued and softened, as the body was solemnly lowered into its resting-place.

A horizontal slab was placed over the grave, on which was an inscription, that has since been lost. The precise place of burial at length became doubtful. But it seemed ungrateful that

Harvard's first President, "the skilful Palinurus, who had guided its first fourteen dubious years with so wise a hand, should lie within the enclosures of its own burying-ground, in an unknown grave;"[1] and accordingly, in the year 1846, special search was made for the spot, and a new monument was reared to Mr. Dunster's memory. The discovery of the grave was an occasion of much interest, and we are happy to give an account of it, written not long after, by a beloved sister of the author, the late Mrs. H. C. Conant, after a visit to Cambridge. She says: "The first effort was fruitless, and the attempt was abandoned. Fortunately, among those interested in the matter, was one of those keen antiquarians, who delight in nothing so much as in a puzzling hunt of this kind. This was Mr. Sibley, the courteous librarian of Harvard College, from whom we obtained an account of the circumstances of the discovery. Assuming that Dunster lay somewhere within the enclosure, he settled it in his own mind that it could be in no other than a certain spot, indicated as follows: first, the tombs of the two Presidents next suc-

[1] Mrs. Conant's Letter.

ceeding Dunster — Chauncy and Oakes — were distinguished from all the other monuments by an upper slab of a peculiar kind of stone imported from England; and, not far from these, partially raised on a heap of loose stones, lay a slab exactly similar, except that the space for the inscription was hollowed out, apparently to give place for a tablet of lead — a practice common at that time. These three stones being the only ones of this peculiar and expensive kind, and two of them appropriated to early Presidents of the College, the third could scarcely be supposed to mark any grave but that of Dunster. This was Mr. Sibley's first point. The second seemed to make it absolutely sure, viz. that in a line with the stone heap thus distinguished, were the graves of two of Dunster's grandchildren, whose names are yet plainly legible on the low headstones. Here then, if anywhere, he felt certain would be found the remains of the first President.

"The slab being laid aside, the loose stones which were heaped some two feet above the surface, were found also to extend downward, filling a cavity of the usual depth of a grave. These being removed, the workmen came upon a stone slab, much decomposed, so as to scale off readily in handling. Under this was a brick enclosure, sufficiently large to admit a coffin, whose tiers were so laid, — the lower ones cross-wise and the upper ones lengthwise, — as to leave a ledge for the support of the slab. The whole interior space was packed with tansy, among which were seen scales of lamp-black paint from the coffin, fragments of a shroud, and — sole remnant of the mortal body once deposited therein — a skull, well covered with auburn hair. But was it Dunster's? On this point there could have been no doubt, but for one circumstance. His death occurred in mid-winter, while the tansy which had been used for the preservation ["embalming"] of the body, being in flower, indicated the warm season. This seemed for a time to defy explanation. The link was at last supplied by a friend living on the Connecticut, who informed Mr. Sibley, that it was there the custom to cut the tansy while in blossom, and hang it up in bunches, for use through the year. The unusual interval, in this case, between the decease and the interment sufficiently accounted for the quantity employed, though in the heart of winter.

"The good man's remains were reverently covered up again; and over them was erected by the Trustees of the University, a plain monument, surmounted by that same ancient slab appropriated to the purpose two hundred years ago. The missing lead tablet, supposed to have done service for the country in the shape of Revolutionary bullets, was replaced by a more enduring one of stone, and an elegant Latin inscription from the classic pen of Mr. Charles Folsom, records the virtues of the dead, and his services to the cause of learning and religion." [1]

[1] "His grave, in the old 'God's Acre' near the halls of Harvard College, was opened July 1, 1846, when the President and Fellows renewed the tablet over it. The remains were found lying, six feet below the surface, in a brick vault which was covered with irregularly-shaped flagstones of slate about three inches thick. The coarse cotton or linen shroud which enveloped them had apparently been saturated with some substance, probably resinous, which prevented it from closely fitting the body. Between it and the remains of the coffin was found a large quantity of common tansy, in seed, a portion of which had evidently been pulled up by the roots. The skeleton appeared to be that of a person of middle size; but it was not measured, as the extremities of the bones of the arms and thighs

"There is," to quote further from the same writer, "something extremely touching in the character and fate of Dunster. One never thinks of pitying such a man as Roger Williams. The prophet fire in his bones, which compels him to cry aloud and spare not, is at the same time an inward witness that his work shall not be in vain; and well may he bravely work and bravely suffer, who knows that he is thus sent on a special errand in the service of truth. But Henry Dunster was not born to be a Reformer. An enthusiast in book-learning, gentle, courteous, affectionate in temper, his natural place was among the conservatives of society. When such a man is forced, by his simple fidelity to

had perished, as well as portions of the cancellated structures of these and of some other bones. The configuration of the skull, which was in good preservation, was such as to the phrenologists indicates qualities, both moral and intellectual, of a superior order. The hair, which appeared to have retained its proper place, was long behind, covering thickly the whole head, and coming down upon the forehead. This, as well as the beard, which upon the upper lip and chin was about half an inch long, was of a light brown color. The eyebrows were thick and nearly met each other." Palfrey, Hist. New England, II. 534, note.

truth, into the lists of a great practical struggle, he is almost sure to be crushed. John Cotton was very much such a man; and he too would have been crushed, but for one gift which was wanting to Dunster,—ability of being convinced by the majority. It was just this difference which saved Cotton his pulpit, and cost Dunster his chair. But after all, I reckon Dunster the more fortunate, as well as the nobler of the two; for his name has come down to us as pure as light, while Cotton kept his place to become the defender of religious persecution."

Cotton Mather, who lived in the second generation after Dunster, has done better justice to him than to Roger Williams; for while, "as a kind of small punishment for Mr. Williams' sins, [he] has left his name out from that remarkable list of ministers . . . who were in the ministry in the Old World before coming to these shores," and has "coupled" him "in the same chapter with the notorious Samuel Gorton;"[1] he has assigned Mr. Dunster a place among those worthies, and the still higher honor of bearing "his part in everlasting celestial hallelujahs." "If," he writes,

[1] Rev. I. N. Tarbox, D.D., *New Englander*, April, 1871.

"unto the Christian, while singing of psalms on earth, Chrysostom could well say, 'Those art in a consort with angels!' how much more may that *now* be said of our Dunster."

APPENDIX.

APPENDIX.

I.

GENEALOGY OF THE DUNSTER FAMILY.

Prepared by Mr. Samuel Dunster, Attleboro', Mass., and his son, Edward S. Dunster, M.D., of New York.

REV. HENRY DUNSTER,[1] first President of Harvard College, was born in Lancashire, England, probably about the year 1610. He was married to ELIZABETH GLOVER, relict of Jesse Glover, about the first of July, 1641.

She died Aug. 23, 1643, without issue by him.

He married a second wife, ELIZABETH (surname unknown), who died "12^{d} 7^{m}, 1690, aged 60," as shown by the Cambridge Records. She came from England, as tradition has it, when about eighteen years of age.

[1] From a document in President Dunster's handwriting, now in the possession of Mr. Samuel Dunster, we have obtained a specimen of his signature:

Henry Dunster:

Mr. Dunster died, in Scituate, Mass., Feb. 27, 1658–9.

Children of Henry Dunster and Elizabeth.

I. DAVID, born at Cambridge, May 16, 1645; died —

II. DOROTHY, born at Cambridge, Jan. 29, 1647–8; died in infancy, probably.

III. HENRY, born at Cambridge, 1650; died in infancy, probably.

IV. JONATHAN, born at Cambridge, Sept. 28, or Oct. 27, 1653; died 1725.

V. ELIZABETH, born at Cambridge, Dec. 29, 1656.

NOTES.

I. DAVID. Nothing is known of him after he was seventeen years of age. He is mentioned in his father's will, at which time he was thirteen. In the Rev. Isaiah Dunster's family Bible, now in the possession of the writer, is this entry in his own handwriting: —

"The children of this President were, I. *Henry*, who returned to England, and, as ye family tradition is, died without issue, a lawyer in Gray's Inn." If Rev. Isaiah Dunster (Pres. Dunster's great-grandchild) mistook this name for David's, as he might very naturally have done, it would explain the want of further knowledge of Pres. D.'s oldest son.

IV. JONATHAN married, Dec. 5, 1678, Abigail Elyott, who died, probably in Charlestown, whither they had removed about 1681. He married a second wife, Mrs. Ruth

Eaton, who survived him, and married, Nov. 22, 1732, Lieut. Amos. Marrett, of Cambridge.

V. ELIZABETH is mentioned in her father's will.

Children of Jonathan Dunster and Abigail Elyott.

I. HENRY,[1] born at Cambridge, July 17, 1680; married Martha Russell, Feb. 25, 1707; died Jan. 28, 1753. This date of his death is from the Bible of his son Jason. In the probate office at East Cambridge his death is recorded in 1748. He and his wife were among the constituent members of the 2d church in Cambridge, now the 1st Congregational Church at Arlington.

II. ELIZABETH, born at Cambridge, Feb. 22, 1681–2; married Philip Carteret, or Cartwright, a mariner of Boston, Nov. 16, 1727.

III. JONATHAN, born at Charlestown, Mass; died in 1742, without issue, and left by will his property to his brothers and sisters.

IV. THOMAS, born at Charlestown, Mass., and is mentioned in the agreement between the heirs of Jonathan Dunster, April 1, 1728, as having lately deceased.

[1] It is recorded to his honor that he brought wood *gratis* to his pastor for seven years.

Continuation of Children of Jonathan Dunster and Abigail Elyott.

V. DOROTHY, married April 13, 1732, to Solomon Page, of Hampton, N.H.

VI. DAVID, born in Charlestown, 1705. In 1726, shortly after their father's decease, a guardian was appointed for David, he being at that time "a Minor in his twentyeth year of age." It is from *this* David that the family of Dunsters in Westminster, Mass., have sprung.

(See list at the end, page 251.)

Children of Henry Dunster and Martha Russell.

I. MARTHA, baptized at Cambridge, Feb. 13, 1708–9; died —, 1800.

II. MARY, baptized at Cambridge, July 13, 1712; died at Mason, N.H., June 29, 1795.

III. ABIGAIL, baptized at Cambridge, Mar. 21, 1713–14.

IV. ELIZABETH. Died Nov. 7, 1716 or 1717.

V. ISAIAH, born at Cambridge, Nov. 1, 1720; died Jan. 18, 1791.

VI. HENRY, born Feb. 17, 1722–23.

VII. JASON, born July 24, 1726; died Feb. 19, 1805.

VIII. RUTH, baptized Oct. 7, 1733; died June 30, 1735.

NOTES.

I. MARTHA married Edward Dickson, March 18, 1730–31.

II. MARY married Amos Marrett, of Cambridge, Sept. 21, 1732. This Marrett was the son of Lieut. Amos Marrett, who married the widow of Jonathan Dunster in 1732.

III. ABIGAIL married a Mr. Cutter.

V. ISAIAH graduated at Harvard College in 1741. Nov. 2, 1748, he was ordained colleague pastor with Rev. Nath. Stone, at Harwich, Mass. He married at Yarmouth, May 26, 1750, Hannah Dennis of that place, who was born Oct. 15, 1730, N.S. She died May 22, 1766, and on the 13th of November following he married, at Pembroke, Mary Smith, born at Yarmouth, May 29, 1735, N.S., who survived him, and died Dec. 23, 1796.

VI. HENRY is mentioned in his father's will, Oct. 1, 1848, as lately deceased. His wife's name was Abigail. He died childless.

VII. JASON married Nov. 6, 1749, Rebecca Cutter. She was born March 19, 1734. He removed to Mason, N.H., in 1769, the next year after the incorporation of the Town, and was, with eleven others, the founder of the First Congregational Church there, Oct. 13, 1772. In the Covenant it is stated, that, "as to matters of faith, we cordially adhere to the principles of religion (at least, the substance of them) contained in the Shorter Catechism of the Assembly of Divines, . . . not as supposing that there is any *authority*, much less *infallibility*, in these human creeds, yet, believing that these principles are drawn from and agreeable to the Scripture, . . . hereby declaring our utter Dislike of the Arminian Principles vulgarly so called."

These children were all born in Cambridge, or Menotomy in West Cambridge.

Children of Isaiah Dunster and Hannah Dennis and Mary Smith.	I. MARTHA (by 1st wife), born Oct. 7, 1763; died Dec. 19, 1808. II. HANNAH (by 2d wife), born Feb. 26, 1768; died at Pembroke, Mass., May 19, 1853. III. JUDITH MILLER, born Dec. 6, 1769; died March 22, 1843. IV. MARY, born May 17, 1772; died April 27, 1850. V. CATHERINE, born March 1, 1774; died May 1, 1811. VI. ABIGAIL, born July 29, 1776; died May 13, 1816.

Probably all born at Harwich.

NOTES.

I. Martha married Dr. James Foster, of Rochester, Mass. Neither of the five other daughters was married. By the death of Hannah, in 1853, this branch of the family became extinct. She was the recipient of the generosity of Harvard College, and bestowed on its library the

Bible of President Dunster. She also in 1852 gave to Edward S. Dunster, at that time a student in Harvard College, now a physician in New York City, the original letters of Prest. Dunster, since published by the Mass. Historical Soc., Vol. II., 4th series, one of which was from his father, Henry Dunster, dated Balehoult (Bury, Lancashire, England), 20th March, 1640.

Children of Jason Dunster and Rebecca Cutter.

I. RUTH, born at Cambridge, Aug. 21, 1750; died at Mason, N.H.

II. REBECCA, born at Cambridge, Aug. 18, 1752; died at Cambridge, June 5, 1753.

III. HENRY, born at Cambridge, Aug. 4, 1754; died in or near Boston, 1794.

IV. REBECCA, born at Cambridge, June 18, 1756; died at Mason, N.H., Aug. 3, 1811.

V. MARTHA, born at Cambridge, Aug. 28, 1758; died at Nelson, N.H., Sept. 3, 1838.

VI. ISAIAH, born at Cambridge, April 10, 1761; died at Roxbury, 1815.

VII. JASON, born at Cambridge, March 27, 1763; died at Mason, N.H., March 21, 1828.

VIII. SAMUEL CUTTER, born at Cambridge, April 20, 1766; died at Ashburnham, Mass., 1840.

NOTES.

I. RUTH married Joseph Blood, born in Groton, Mass., July 29, 1743, who was killed at the battle of Bunker Hill. They had four children.

III. HENRY lived in Mason from 1769 till about 1780. He did service in the Revolutionary War. Went to Brookline, Mass., where he married, as tradition says, a Miss Sharp, and died leaving two children, *twins*, Henry and Sally, who were born March 25, 1782 (this is certain). Sally was given to her Aunt Wright at Packersfield, now Nelson, Mass. She died April 22, 1808, at the house of her aunt. She was unmarried.

IV. REBECCA married John Swallow, of Mason, N.H.

V. MARTHA married Oliver Wright, of Nelson, N.H., Sept. 7, 1783.

VI. ISAIAH married Miss Davis, of Roxbury, and died childless. He owned the hotel between Boston and Dedham, called the "Punch Bowl." He did service in the Revolutionary War.

VII. JASON married, April 18, 1793, Polly Merriam, of Mason, N.H., who was born Oct. 28, 1768. At the age of sixteen he enlisted into the Continental Army, from Lexington or Cambridge, and served four years, until the close of the war, and was honorably discharged by Gen. Knox. He received a Revolutionary pension. His widow also received a pension till her death, May 4, 1858.

VIII. SAMUEL CUTTER married Hannah Townsend, of

Mason, N.H. (born in Northborough, Mass.), Jan. 12, 1792, and removed to Ashburnham, Mass., where he introduced the spinning of cotton by machinery. His wife died about 1822. He afterwards married her sister Madimoisella (called Madie). They had no children.

Children of Henry Dunster and Sally Sharp (?).	HENRY and SALLY, twins, born March 25, 1782. Sally died unmarried at Nelson, Mass., April 22, 1808. Henry married Rhoda Jackson, who was born in 1778, at Bridgewater, Mass., and lived in South Street, Boston, where he died of consumption, July 9, 1813. Buried at Roxbury Neck.
Children of Jason Dunster and Polly Merriam.	I. JASON, born at Mason, N.H., July 15, 1794. Now (1872) living at Westport, New York. II. MARY, born at Mason, N.H., Feb. 16, 1796; died at Mason, May 31, 1864. III. ISAIAH, born Dec. 10, 1798; died at Attleboro', Mass., Aug. 4, 1857. IV. BETSEY, born April 20, 1801. Now (1872) living at Mason, N.H. V. SAMUEL (the writer of this genealogy), born Aug. 1, 1803. VI. REBECCA, born Sept. 25, 1805; died at Mason, June 25, 1810. VII. JULIANNA, born Feb. 21, 1808; died by fall from a bed, July 21, 1808.

NOTES.

I. JASON married Azubah Felt, of Temple, N.H., Oct. 22, 1816. She died Oct. 23, 1819, and he married Hannah Hardy, of Westport, N.Y., Jan. 19, 1823. He served in the war of 1812, as an ensign, and was stationed at Portsmouth, N.H. For this service he receives a pension from the United States.

II. MARY married, Dec. 25, 1815, Benoni C. Kimball, of Mason, who died 1868.

III. ISAIAH married Ruth Sophia Fisk, of Waltham, Mass., Feb. 6, 1823. Died at Attleboro', Mass., Aug. 4, 1857.

IV. BETSEY married Moses Russell, of Mason, Aug. 27, 1819. Now resides in Mason.

V. SAMUEL married Susan Perkins Dow, of Rochester, N.H. Is a machinist and calico printer. Now (1872) lives in Attleboro', Mass.

Children of Henry Dunster and Rhoda Jackson.

I. SARAH, born Dec. 28, 1808; married Joseph Ferrin, July 28, 1833.

II. HENRY JACKSON, born Sept. 24, 1810. About 1818 learned the printer's trade. He married Mary B. Savery, of Plymouth, Mass., who was born Aug. 23, 1813. Went South for his health; died July 7, 1839, and was buried at Georgetown, S.C.

Continuation of Children of Henry Dunster and Rhoda Jackson.

III. WILLIAM, born April 22, 1812; died at sea, 1830.

IV. RHODA, died in infancy, 1813.

V. JANE LYDIA DAMON, born Jan. 22, 1815; married Charles Johnston, July 13, 1834; he died about seven years ago. She is now (1872) living at 763 Broadway, South Boston.

VI. EPHRAIM JACKSON, born May 22, 1817; died Sept. 9, 1817.

All born in Boston.

Children of Jason Dunster and Azubah Felt and Hannah Hardy.

I. HENRY JASON (by 1st wife), born at Mason, N.H., Sept. 19, 1817; died June 26, 1857, at Westport, N.Y.

II. AZUBAH FELT (by 2d wife), b. Westport, Sept. 14, 1823; d., June 2, 1849, unm.

III. PHEBE LOUISA, born at Westport, Sept. 6, 1825.

IV. SARAH, b. at Westport, Sept. 8, 1828.

V. CHARLES CARROL, b. Westport, March 19, 1830. Now liv. in Westport, N.Y.

VI. SAMUEL K., born at Westport, Aug. 11, 1832. Now living in Philadelphia.

VII. ISAIAH HARDY, b. Westport, Feb. 28, 1835. Unm. Living in Camanche, Ia.

VIII. MARY MERRIAM, born at Westport, Nov. 4, 1837. Unmarried.

IX. ELLERY G., b. Westport, Jan. 8, 1844; died, Dec. 11, 1848, of scarlatina.

NOTES.

I. HENRY JASON married Martha Percil, born June 21, 1820, at Westport, N.Y., Nov. 7, 1840.

III. PHEBE L. married Morris Sherman, of Westport, May 10, 1849.

IV. SARAH married Wait P. Bristol, of Westport, May 30, 1848.

V. CHARLES CARROL, married Rachel Benson, of Westport, March 19, 1860.

VI. SAMUEL K. married Elizabeth J. Wallace, born March 10, 1843, at Sandwich, N.H., Oct. 16, 1860. She died Nov. 16, 1866. He was in the 24th Regt. Mass. Vol., and served to the close of the war.

VII. ISAIAH HARDY enlisted in the 8th Regt. of Iowa Volunteers soon after the secession of the Southern States. Was taken prisoner at the battle of Shiloh. After being transported through most of the Southern States, he was exchanged and joined his regiment. Was commissioned captain, and raised a company of colored troops.

Children of Isaiah Dunster and Sophia Fisk.

I. ELIZA SOPHIA, born at Waltham, Mass., April 5, 1824; died Aug. 7, 1866.

II. HENRY, born at New Ipswich, N.H., April 13, 1831.

NOTES.

I. ELIZA married Moses Mason, of Attleboro', Mass., and died Aug. 7, 1866.

II. HENRY married Jane Mellen, of Providence, R.I., (who was born Feb. 3, 1831), Oct. 6, 1851. He now lives in Providence.

Children of Samuel Dunster and Susan P. Dow.

I. MARY SUSAN, born at Dover, N.H., Aug. 9, 1830; died at Bustleton, Pa., June 27, 1832.

II. MARY SUSAN, born at Bustleton, Pa., June 27, 1833.

III. EDWARD SWIFT, born at Sanford, Me., Sept. 2, 1834.

IV. CALEB EMERY, born at Sanford, Me., July 27, 1836; died at Sanford, Oct. 7, 1836.

V. ELIZA ANNIE, born at Durham, N.H., Oct. 24, 1838.

NOTES.

II. MARY SUSAN mar. I. E. Smith, of Durham, N.H., Dec. 25, 1849. Had two children; both died in infancy.

III. EDWARD S. was prepared for college in Providence High School; entered Harvard College Sept., 1852, and graduated 1856; graduated at New York Medical College 1858, with the highest honors; appointed surgeon in the army 1861; was medical director of the hospital transports in the Peninsular campaign; surgeon at West Point; and is now Professor of Obstetrics and Diseases of Women and Children in the University of Vermont, and also at the Long Island College Hospital, in Brooklyn, N.Y. Is editor of "The New York Medical Journal," and superintendent of Infants' Hospital, New York.

He married Rebecca Morgan Sprole, daughter of Rev. Dr. Sprole, of Newburgh, N.Y., Nov. 4, 1863. She was born in Philadelphia, Pa., Nov. 6, 1835.

V. ELIZA ANNIE graduated with high honor at Bradford Academy, at Bradford, Mass., and also attended Mrs. Willard's Seminary at Troy. She taught in Chicago, and also at Amitie Seminary in Mississippi.

She married William T. Baker, of Chicago, July 4, 1861, where she now lives, having had five children, four of whom are now living.

Children of Henry Dunster and Mary B. Savary.

I. HENRY JACKSON, born at Charlestown, Mass., Oct. 7, 1834; he died Jan. 1, 1835.

II. ANDREW JACKSON, born in Boston, Nov. 30, 1836. After the death of their third child and the death of her husband, his widow, Mary B. Savary, changed the name of Andrew Jackson, their second child, to Henry Jackson, to perpetuate the name of President Dunster, believing that this child was the *only* male descendant alive!

III. HENRY JACKSON, b. at Plymouth, Aug., 1838; died there Sept. 5, 1839.

NOTE.

II. HENRY JACKSON (2d) married Marianna Brewster (a descendant of "Elder" Brewster) Jan. 1, 1857. She was born Aug., 1837. Now living in Duxbury, Mass.

<table>
<tr><td rowspan="7">Children of Henry Dunster and Martha Percil.</td><td>I. ELIZA E., born Dec. 15, 1841.</td></tr>
<tr><td>II. LUCIUS F., born Aug. 22, 1843. Died Dec. 9, 1848, of scarlatina.</td></tr>
<tr><td>III. WHEATON HENRY, born Nov. 26, 1845; died Dec. 23, 1848, of scarlatina.</td></tr>
<tr><td>IV. MYRON N., born Jan. 9, 1848; died Dec. 17, 1848, of scarlatina.</td></tr>
<tr><td>V. HARRIET M., born Oct. 23, 1849; died May 10, 1865.</td></tr>
<tr><td>VI. WHEATON HENRY, born Oct. 11, 1852.</td></tr>
<tr><td>VII. ATHELIA S., born Jan. 1, 1855.</td></tr>
</table>

All born in Westport, N.Y.

<table>
<tr><td>Child of Charles Carroll Dunster and Rachel Benson.</td><td>I. CLARA, born Dec. 23, 1867.</td></tr>
</table>

Child of Samuel K. Dunster and Elizabeth J. Wallace.

I. Charles Kimball, born March 23, 1861.

Children of Henry Dunster and Jane Mellen.

I. Ida Louisa, born at Attleboro', Mass., Sept. 25, 1852.

II. Henry, born at Providence, R.I., May 25, 1857.

Children of Henry Dunster and Marianna Brewster.

I. Henry Loyd, born at Duxbury, Mass., Dec. 24, 1857.

II. Louisa Ann, born at Duxbury, Mass., March 28, 1861.

III. Elizabeth Watson, born at Duxbury, Mass., Nov. 30, 1864.

IV. Jane Johnson, born at Duxbury, Mass., Dec. 24, 1866.

Children of Edward Swift Dunster and Rebecca M. Sprole.

I. CLARA BERTRAM, born Dec. 19, 1865, at West Point, N.Y.

II. WILLIAM SPROLE, born Nov. 20, 1867, at New York City; died at Newburgh, N.Y., July 13, 1868.

III. ELIZABETH MORGAN, born Aug. 25, 1870, at Infants' Hospital, New York City, of which her father is Superintendent.

Record of the Descendants of David Dunster, the sixth child of Jonathan Dunster (son of President Dunster), and Abigail Ellyott, born in Charlestown.

In 1741, Dec. 2, he drew Home lot No. 10 of Narragansett, No. 2, and was the third settler of Westminster, Mass. The line of descent — as given by Mrs. Emma C. Dunster, the second wife of Martin Dunster, M.D., and also by Mrs. Daupheny Leland Dunster Parsons, who was the youngest sister of Dr. Martin D., was as follows: —

HENRY DUNSTER, President H.C.
JONATHAN (omitted by them. S.D.)
DAVID.
HUBBARD.
HUBBARD.
MARTIN.

Children of David Dunster and Molly Russel.	I. BETTY.
	II. MARGERY.
	III. HUBBARD.
	IV. MOLLY.
	V. THOMAS.
	VI. RUHAMA.
	VII. HENRY.

NOTES.

I. HUBBARD married Ruth Bailey Aug. 31, 1769.

V. THOMAS married Lidia Pierce, of Fitchburg, Mass., Feb., 1768.

VII. HENRY married Anna Pierce, of Leominster, Nov., 1778.

Children of Hubbard and Ruth Bailey.	I. HUBBARD.
	II. EPHRAIM.
	III. REBECKAH.
	IV. JASON.
	V. NATHAN.
	VI. JONATHAN.

NOTE.

I. HUBBARD married, May 1, 1797, Becca Kendall, of Gardner.

Children of Thomas and Lidia.	I. DAVID. II. KEZIAH. III. ANNA. IV. THOMAS. V. LYDIA. IV. PRECILLA; married —— ESTERBROOK.
Children of Hubbard Dunster and Becca.	I. MARTIN. He was born Jan. 3, 1798; he married Sally Nichols for his 1st wife, Feb. 13, 1823; died in Quincy, Ill., Dec. 2, 1854. Was twice married, but left no heirs. II. PRUDA, born Jan. 23, 1800; married Isaac Fitts, Jr., 1818. III. REBECKAH, born Feb. 11, 1802. IV. LOUISA, born Feb. 18, 1805. V. ASAPH, born July 6, 1807, was living in 1860 at Quincy, Ill. VI. MARY JANE, born Nov. 12, 1809. VII. LYDIA, born Jan. 24, 1816. VIII. DAUPHENY LELAND, born July 18, 1818.

See *Willard Memoir* (pp. 346–350), by Joseph Willard, for notices of Dunsters in England.

1595, y[e] 10 Auguste, baptised Henry, son of Willime Dunsture.

1617, 10 October, married Henry Dunster and Isabell Kay.

1618, Jan'y vij° [7th], baptised Mary, daughter of Henry Dunster minor.

1619, Aprill xxij° [22d], baptised Elisabeth, daughter of Henry Dunster.

1620, November xxix [29th], baptised Henry, son of Henry Dunster.

1622, May 4, baptised John, son of Henry Dunster, of Elton.

1625, Auguste 8, baptised Daniell, son of Henry Dunster, of Eltoun.

1627, December 27, baptised Alice, daughter of Henrie Dunster, of Elton.

1632, July 15th, baptised Elisab, daughter of Henry Dunster, of Elton.

1635, Aprill 26, baptised James, son of Henry Dunster, of Elton.

1637, November 5, baptised Robert, son of Henry Dunster, of Lane.

The foregoing authenticated record, taken from the Parish Register of Bury, was placed at the author's service by the courtesy of Charles Deane, Esq. of Cambridge, Mass., who, when in England, in the year 1854, procured it from Mr. Ra Crompton, Parish Clerk.

A comparison of this record with the notices of the family to which the President belonged, contained in his father's letter (p. 21) and will (p. 303) and in Savage's Gen. Dictionary, will show remarkable points of coincidence. In both the former and the latter, there are a father and son Henry, and a son Robert, and daughters Elisabeth and Mary. The reference in the letter to Elisabeth: "Your sister Elisabeth is turned scribe, and can do very well of three weeks time," — which represents her as having just begun to write, — well agrees with the date of baptism in the register (1632), making her at the date of the letter (1640–1) about eight years old. Supposing the Elisabeth in the register to have been the second wife of Major Willard, she would have been about twenty at the time of her marriage. Major Willard married a Mary Dunster (see Savage, Gen. Dict. Art. Willard) as his third wife.

But against this, is the record in the register, of four children, John, Daniel, Alice and James, not named in the letter. They may have died, however, before the letter was written; and as to Richard and Thomas (named in the letter, but not in the register), we may suppose them to have been born elsewhere; and that the birth of one occurred between the years 1620 and 1622, and that of the other between 1625 and 1627. Alice may have been the name of the daughter (conjecturally, it would seem, named Rose by Savage (Gen. Dict. Art. Hills) who married Captain Joseph Hills. Thomas is spoken of in the letter as a widower, who had lost his wife and children. Supposing him to have been born in 1621, he would be only nineteen at the date of the letter — pretty young to be the father of children. But what is further said of him : "I pray God he take good ways," might well agree with his having entered into a premature marriage.

The early age which the parish register would assign to Henry Dunster for entering College, and afterwards becoming President, — thirteen and twenty, — is a serious difficulty; as is also the mention by President Dunster, in his Christian Experience, of Dr. Preston at Cambridge, he having died in 1628.

It is a curious fact, that two of the sons of Simon Willard by Elisabeth or Mary Dunster were named John and Daniel (see Savage, Gen. Dict.)[1]

[1] From the "Willard Memoir," by Joseph Willard, Boston, 1858, page 345, we copy the following : "'It was clear [says Rev. Mr. Hunter, of England] that Balehoult was some place so called in the neighborhood of Bury of Lancashire, and probably in the parish of Bury.' — 'The Rev. Mr. Hornby, the rector of Bury, in a letter addressed to Rev. Canon Raines says, "There is a place in the township of Elton [thirteen and a quarter miles from Bury] called now Bolholt, which I don't doubt is the place you mean; because there is a house not very far from it which goes by the name of 'Dunster's.' I looked through a good deal of the registers, but I could find no entry of any of the Dunsters." — 'The name of Dunster, however,' says Mr. Hunter, 'is ancient in those parts of Lancashire.' — 'It frequently occurs,' according to Mr. Raines, 'in the register of Middleton (a parish adjoining that of Bury), from the beginning.' — 'It seems probable,' adds Mr. Hunter, 'that the Dunster who wrote the letter [Henry Dunster, father of the President. See page 8,] may have transferred his household from the parish of Middleton to Bury. I am, however, a little surprised at not finding the name in any of our Subsidy Rolls for those parts of the kingdom, since it is evident that they were a family possessed of property, and also of better attainments than most of their neighbors, — belonging, I should say, to the better class of yeomanry.'"

II.

CONFESSION OF FAITH AND CHRISTIAN EXPERIENCE.[1]

Deare brethren and sisters in Christ, I account it no small mercy that the Lord has called me to give an account of that fayth and love I beare to Christ and his Church and people. 1 : Concerning fayth.

1 The summe of [the] Christian religion contaynes fayth and obedience ; as you are dayly taught.

1 Concerning fayth. I hold no fayth which is not grounded on the revealed Word of God in the worlde, the only rule of fayth and manners, so that they are not to be heard though they come as angels from heauen. It teacheth 1 God & 2 Ourselves. 1 Concerning God. We come to knowe him 1. in his essence and persons.

1 Concerning his essence, I believe there is one God, the only maker of all things, who is in himselfe full wise and holy and gracious, every way perfect and sufficient ground of happiness and maine pillar of happiness to his people, so that our spirit can find no adequate object of happiness but God only ; who only can satisfy the spirit, and who hath a world to command. This God so sufficient yet made a world in time by the word of his power, by his holy Word Christ and by his Spirit movinge on the waters to bringe them to forme ; wherein he hath shewn his endless power and bounty.

[1] From a MS. volume in the Library of the Historic Genealogical Society, by Rev. Thomas Shepard, entitled, "The Confessions of Diverse propounded to be received, and were entertained as members."

I also believe he governs the whole world by his Providence, so that no bird or hayre falls but by it.

The spirituall creatures are angels and men. Angels, some are good, and some are bad. Man also by the first temptation of Satan fell from God, and fell from the blessed image of God created in holiness and righteousness, and believinge Satan did receive the character and image of Satan on his soule; and in our naturall state they have communion with the deuill [and] cannot be subject unto the law. Man thus fallinge, God in his mercy comes to seeke man, and when man appeares before his Creator, though first convinced of his guilt, God [imparteth?] out of his mercy, the gospell that the woman's seed shall break the serpent's head; so that God, pityinge our estate, hath sent us a Saviour having 2 natures, one divine, begotten of [the] father before all worlds, the other manly nature because he tooke body and soule, and so are united in one individuall person. God — else he could not satisfy, nor be a sufficient head for the church, to shed his Spirit for the building [his] kingdom. And man because man had sinned, and they that sinned must dy and suffer; hath sanctified our nature in the manhood, and in his person hath perfectly fulfilled [the] law of God and satisfied wrath, and so hath wrought for us full salvation. I need not speake of his judgment, all which I believe as tis in [the] gospell.

Concerning our union to Christ — how we come to Christ. 1 Every man is not partaker of Christ in the visible way in churches many perish all have not lively fayth many shall seeke to enter in and shall not be able though they pretend Christ and fayth ; though I hope better in such churches where we are made partakers of Christ by fayth only, which fayth is not [the] foundation, every persuasion is not Christ, but lively stickinge to God and Christ for life, and is ordinarily wrought by the word of fayth, and hence let those that do not believe attend on [the] word of fayth. This fayth which God worketh in men's hearts, he doth dayly strengthen by those ordinances in his church, especially by [the] word — hence not as some erringe ones cast off the word of fayth to receive suggestions and revelations without limit, which is provoking God to take away all the Spirit: The Spirit teacheth only ordinarily in God's ordinances ; hence give not eare to them that looke only to be fed by heaven castinge off ordinances.

As [the] word, so Prayer is another means to confirm fayth. Pray to the Lord, and when ye do pray, believe, and so this will strengthen fayth.

As prayer, so the Lord hath given 2 sacraments.

1. Baptisme, by which we have our initiation, and concerning it I believe that only believers and their seed ought to be received into the church by that sacrament. Hence prophane unbelievers are not to be received into the church ; and then their seed are [not] to be received. That of Paul is cleare. Else your children were unholy —hence if holy, let them be offered to God. Let children come to me, and as children, so those that come to mature age ought to be received into the church by bap-

tisme. And concerning the outward elements something there is concerning sprinkling in the Scriptures — hence not offended when [it] is used.

You that have been baptised and have made a covenant in baptisme to forsake the devill, away then with pride, [the] world, and lust of [the] flesh, hence live not in licentiousness &c: and your covenant is to believe in Christ for life — hence give up yourselves to Christ — so for obedience.

2. The other sacrament is the Lord's Supper — the outward elements bread and wine. And 'tis not the quantity of the elements which our soules neede, but fayth in which we receive. Outward elements may be given when Christ is not, and grace may be given when sacraments are not; for though we have not sacraments every day, yet we may have communion with Christ, and let those that be kept out humble themselves, so that it be not contemned. And here let me protest against the wickednesse of Papists, who thinke Christ is bodily present — Faith only makes present. Now altars & tables have no fayth. But we receive Christ spiritually. 3 Holy Conferences. 4 Dayly reading the Scriptures. 5 The private ordinances of soliloquys and meditations. 6 Discipline in the church. [The] Lord hath commanded there should be a difference betweene [the] precious and the vile. Hence 2 sorts should be held out 1 unbelievers 2 disobedient, for all Christian religion contayneth fayth and obedience, the soule and body of the church. Hence if he sayth he hath fayth and hath no obedience, ought to be kept out. If obedient without fayth, i.e. walkes civilly only, he ought to be kept out,

and hence this keeping forth is holy, just and good, and [I] shall labour to my power to maintayne. Nay, if those that do believe and obey, yet if they walk ill, are to be admonished. If they reforme, blesse God ; but if they do not reforme, then [take] two or three more, and so, at last cast out, and afterwards to be received if they repent — hence I blesse God to see this.

7 There are also extraordinary helps to help the fayth and obedience and [for] your sins — as Fasting and Prayer in case of general calamity ; and so with any speciall thanksgiving to feast in God's presence with all moderation and if the Lord do pursue our spirits with some speciall benefits, a Christian may vow part of his substance or indearment [indeavor ?] to God, which ought to be performed.

2 Obedience to God which follows from fayth ; for fayth being in the heart is not concealed, but its effectuall to cleanse the heart from sin, and to advance his soule with grace, so that he desires to be holy as Christ is holy. Now here they fall from fayth who hold they believe, but they may live dissolutely. These are worse than the devills ; for a Christian takes Christ's righteousness and holiness to kill the old man — sanctify as well as justify, to save you from the guilt of sin on your conscience, and power of sin in your heart. Papists, the contrary, thinke to be saved by their own doings and labor for sanctification. With this last I hope we shall not be pestered, because [the] Lord is bruising his power, but let us in this country looke to the other.

The guide of their holiness, or the touchstone by which 'tis tryed is generally by [the] word, particularly by Law, which Law we receive not from Moses out of Christ, but from Christ writing those Laws on our hearts by the finger of the Holy Ghost. Now this Law is administered either in the letter, and so convinceth of grosse sins, — and in the spirit; and so he is convicted of idolatry when he loves the creature, he is convicted of sabbath [breaking ?] and disobedience to parents, and when he hath any rebellious thoughts — and so far breaking the commandments; the thought is against the commandments.

A Christian having led his life in christian obedience, I believe the Lord at death will take him to himself at death and judgment, when all Christ's enemys shall be trod under his feet; when God [shall say] Ye cursed; and when he cometh our bodies and soules shall be made like unto him.

Concerninge the Lord's personall dealings with my soule. David saith, I will declare thy truth to the greate congregation — hence I do speake.

There was a servant of God, Mr. Hubbard, powerfull. I was not past 4 or 5 yeare old: I heard many scoff at his preachinge, at this great flocking after him, and I asked why men did so. They said, to heare the word, and I said then, if it be the word, why do men speake against it; if it be not, why do men heare it? but I went no further. But about 12 years old, [the] Lord gave us a minister, and the Lord gave me an attentive eare, and heart to understand preachinge out of Revela[tion]. Repent, else they could not be saved. And whereof they should repent, of the sins shewn out of the Law. This word was more sweet to me than anything in the world, and hence some tooke notice of me, and labored to set on the word by confirmation. The Lord showed me my sins, and reconciliation by Christ, and to believe, and when I heare and to obey. But with many faylings in the schoole. I remembered this worke well. After this I went to Cambridge, where, growing more careless, I lost my comfort. But I came to Trinity to heare Dr. Preston,[1] by which I was quickened and revived, so that the word did follow. But especially Mr. Goodwin out of Ps. 85, I was convinced I had departed from God by folly in dissolute living, and hence I thought if [I] lived unto God, the Lord would speake peace ; if not, e contra. A moneth [month] after, my heart did fall off to folly ; and the greatest thing which separated my soule from God was [an] inordinate love of humane learning. Take heed of this least desiring to be as gods, we become as devills. When I came from [the] University to teach schoole, the Lord wounded my soule with temptations for [5 ?] years together. One in this country seeing me fall in such weakness spoke peacably. But in every thing the Lord showed me my faylings, so that reading Rom. 1 and Gal. 5, I saw all the abominations of [the] Gentiles, even to kill parents ; I [was ?] showed I did steale ; in stealing from parents ; so that the Lord showed me how I did so live in every

[1] See page 12.

sin, and I saw I did leave a steyne on every ordinance of God. The more I did strive to keep the Law, the more vile I felt myself. And hence I thought, thou hast returned to folly, and hence I speake everlasting wrath to thee. I saw nothing but doleful horror in [the] conscience, and looked when lightnings should kill me — ear open and mind apt to all errors — memory could retayne no good, and so in [the] affections, and heart unthinkably and inconceivably hard. And at last the Lord showed me where the fault was, that is, that I sought righteousness by the Law. In my judgment I sought salvation by Christ, but indeed did not; but Rom. 10, beginning, the Lord shewed [me] the Jewes fell on that stumbling-stone. And here the Lord 1 informed 2 persuaded my mind, that I could never have my reconciliation and cleansing but by [the] righteousness and spirit of his Son.

But here I found another obstacle — will the Lord have mercy on such an enemy; Hence the Lord, Rom. 5 : 8, 9, 10, the Lord shewed me that while enemys Christ dyed for the ungodly; and hence I saw there was not only righteousness in Christ, but even for those that were sinners, and saw themselves enemys & in feares here I read the Psalm 40, where every verse tooke an impression on my soule; I waited patiently, do so, and I in [the] miry pit, and set me on rock. So I saw [the] Lord could do so for me, and when I saw no offering was required but boring the eare, I saw the Lord must enable me to heare, whereupon I come; as Christ, and of David, and so might be verifyed of every member of Christ. And I desired

[the] Lord would write his Lawes ; and I saw innumerable evills had compassed me about, yet as David thought, Now is a time, I was enabled to gather sure 'tis a time for me to call upon the Lord. And herein the Lord answered me, Looke up to the Lord to be reconciled, and change my nature. I believe the word, [the] Lord would receive an enemy; but I did not discourse, Am I such an enemy as feels it? because I did really feele it. Hence I thought, he that is such an enemy [the] Lord might receive. Hence I cast my soule on [the] Lord's grace & then I bid adeu to all [self] righteousness. When thus I let go my hold of all that, and took hold on Christ [the] Lord I did believe, and hence love [the] Lord.

A man may not only see he is a sinner, and so thinke Christ will receive such a one, but here may be a deceipt, for a man must hold on waitinge till [the] Lord speake peace. Hence in such cases, stay and waite on the Lord, and though you do believe the promise, stay for the Spirit till he seales the promise &c. [The] Lord hath made me bid adieu to all worldly treasures ; and as corruptions in the Church came 1 I began to suspect them, then to hate them. But here was my falsenes that I was loath to read such books as might make me see such truths, but the Lord helped me among all.

So, after 10 years troubles, I came hither ; and the Lord gives me peace to see the order of his people. And I blesse God for keepinge me out, but I desire you to be carefull what schollers enter to your churches, and pray for humility of spirit.

III.

[From "New England's First Fruits," 1642.]

The Times and order of their Studies, unless experience shall shew cause to alter.

The second and third day of the weeke, read Lectures, as followeth.

To the first yeare at 8th of the clock in the morning, Logick, the first three quarters, Physicks the last quarter.

To the second yeare, at the 9th houre, Ethicks and Politicks at convenient distances of time.

To the third yeare, at the 10th, Arithmetick and Geometry, the three first quarters, Astronomy the last.

AFTERNOONE.

The first yeare disputes at the second houre.

The second yeare at the 3d houre.

The third yeare at the 4th, every one in his art.

The 5th day read Greeke.

To the first yeare, the Etymologie and Syntax at the eighth houre.

To the second, at the 9th houre, Prosodia and Dialects.

AFTERNOONE.

The first yeare at 2d houre, practice the precepts of Grammar, in such authors as have variety of words.

The second yeare at 3d houre practice in Poesy, Nounus, Duport, or the like.

The third yeare perfect their Theory before noon, and exercise Style, Composition, Imitation, Epitome, both in prose and verse, afternoone.

The fifth day read Hebrew, and the Easterne Tongues: Grammar to the first yeare, houre the 8th.

To the 2d Chaldee, at the 9th houre.

To the 3d Syriack, at the 10th houre.

AFTERNOONE.

The first yeare practice in the Bible at the 2d houre.

The 2d in Ezra and Daniel at the 3d houre.

The 3d at the 4th houre in Trostius New Testament.

The 6th day read Rhetorick to all at the 8th houre.

Declamations at the 9th. So ordered that every schollar may declaime once a moneth. The rest of the day vacat Rhetoricis studiis.

The 7th day read Divinity Catecheticall at the 8th houre. Common places at the 9th houre.

AFTERNOONE.

The first houre read history in the winter.

The nature of plants in the summer.

The summe of every lecture shall be examined, before the new lecture be read.

Every schollar, that on proofe is found able to read the originals of the Old and New Testament into the Latine tongue, and to resolve them logically; withall being of godly life and conversation; and at any publick act hath the approbation of the Overseers and Master of the Colledge, is fit to be dignified with his first degree.

Every schollar that giveth up in writing a System, or Synopsis, or summe of Logick, naturall and morall Philosophy, Arithmetick, Geometry, and Astronomy, And is ready to defend his Theses or positions: Withall skilled in originalls as above said: And of godly life and conversation: And so approved by the Overseers and Master of the Colledge, at any publique Act, is fit to be dignified with his 2d degree.

IV.

THE THESES OF THE FIRST CLASS OF GRADUATES AT HARVARD COLLEGE, IN 1642.

THESES PHILOLOGICAS.

Grammaticas.

1. Linguarum Scientia est utillissima.
2. Literae non exprimunt quantum vocis organa efferunt.
3. Hebraea est Linguarum Mater.
4. Consonantes et vocales Haebraeorum sunt coetaneae.
5. Punctationes chatephatae syllabam proprie non efficiunt.
6. Linguarum Graeca est copiosissima.
7. Lingua Graeca est ad accentus pronuntianda.
8. Lingua Latina est eloquentissima.

Rhetoricas.

1. Rhetorica specie differt a Logica.
2. In Elocutione perspicuitati cedit ornatus, ornatui copia.
3. Actio primas tenet in pronuntiatione.
4. Oratoris est celare Artem.

Logicas.

1. Universalia non sunt extra intellectum.

2. Omnia Argumenta non sunt relata.
3. Causa *sine qua non* non est peculiaris causa a quatuor reliquis generalibus.
4. Causa et effectus sunt simul tempore.
5. Dissentanea sunt aeque nota.
6. Contrarietas est tantum inter duo.
7. Sublato relato tollitur correlatum.
8. Genus perfectum aequaliter communicatur speciebus.
9. Testimonium valet quantum testis.
10. Elenchorum doctrina in Logica non est necessaria.
11. Axioma contingens est, quod ita rerum est, ut aliquando falsum esse possit.
12. Praecepta Artium debent esse κατὰ πάντος, καθ' ἀυτὸ, καθ' ὅχου πρῶτον.

THESES PHILOSOPHICAS.

Ethicas.

1. Philosophia practica est eruditionis meta.
2. Actio virtutis habitum antecellit.
3. Voluntas est virtutis moralis subjectum.
4. Voluntas est formaliter libera.
5. Prudentia virtutum difficilima.
6. Prudentia est virtus intellectualis et moralis.
7. Justitia mater omnium virtutum.
8. Mors potius subeunda quam aliquid culpae perpetrandum.
9. Non injuste agit nisi qui libens agit.
10. Mentiri potest qui verum dicit.
11. Juveni modestia summum ornamentum.

Physicas.

1. Corpus naturale mobile est subjectum Physicae.
2. Materia secunda non potest existere sine formâ.
3. Forma est accidens.
4. Unius rei non est nisi unica forma constitutiva.
5. Forma est principium individuationis.
6. Privatio non est principium internum.
7. Ex meris accidentibus non fit substantia.
8. Quicquid movetur ab alio movetur.
9. In omni motu movens simul est cum mobili.
10. Coelum non movetur ab intelligentiis.
11. Non dantur orbes in coelo.
12. Quod libet Elementum hæbet unam ex primis qualitatibus sibi maxime propriam.
13. Putredo in humido fit a calore externo.
14. Anima not fit ex traduce.
15. Vehemens sensibile destruit sensum.

Metaphysicas.

1. Omne ens est bonum.
2. Omne creatum est concretum.
3. Quicquid aeternum idem est immensum.
4. Bonum metaphysicum non suscipit gradus.

Hutchinson's Hist. of Mass. I. 510–513.

V.

A COPPY OF MY LR TO DR CHRISTIANUS RAVIUS ORIENTALIŪ LINGUARŪ PFESSOR LONDINI.

REVEREND AND WORTHY SR — Yors of ye 27th of ffebruary came to our hands, together wth the box and all things therein mentioned about the 2d or 3d of August, for wch I am not only bounden to give thanks unto God for raising up such instruments to promote his Kingdome, not onely in the places where they live, but also throughout all the world to the utmost of their power, But I am also further desired from my Occasions in the Colledge to return thanks unto your selfe for yor speciall good will, as to the whole Country here in Generall, so in speciall to the promoting of Learning in the Colledge amongst the Students, and in the woods amongst the Indians in their Savage booths or wigwams; and albeit it extendeth onely to ye power to acknowlege such kindnesse, without further externall requitalls, yet undoubtedly the Lord Jesus takes notice of all his faithfull subjects prayers and endeavors, to enlarge his Kingdome, and will here requite it, wth the perfume of a good name better than pretious oyntment, and hereafter wth a Come yee blessed of my Father inherit the Kingdome. Now for a more speciall answer to the Ten particulars expressed in your letter wee have attended the first in teaching no use of C when the sound thereof is confounded with S or K. But onely where Ch. soundeth, as in our English Language Chaffe,

Cheif, Chose, Chuse, wch sound is frequent in their Language also, in these Kochittuate, Kuchomakin, Mattachuset, wch I pray you inform mee why it may not bee most expedient sound, or power of the letter (ח) Cheth as wee utter it in the word רחל for so I teach for expedience my pupills to pronounce it *διακρίσεως ἕνεκα* least wee should confound it wth ה or ע on the one side, or with כ or ק on the other side. 2^ly whereas you say the letter Q is superfluous in our English, 'tis true the Southern English confound it with K: but wee in the North (Ego enim Lancastrensis sum) pronounce it fully, and exactly as your selfe teach. Orthographiae Hebreae delineationis pag: 5. Col: 1. Sect: 11. of ק Q not K ubi dicis nulli Europaei noverint hujus sonum; praeter Helvetios. Sc. K. ex imo guttere asperius, sic etiam nos efferimus Quod non ut meridionales (Kod). The Indians also have use of this letter frequently in their tongue as in Quillipiog, Quinticut, Quabâquick, &c., wch sound we can never represent by K. | χ indeed there is no need of wth them, but I cannot say so of: Z: wch both their Tongue hath need of in some Syllables, & our owne, ffor the Letter: S: is too dry to expresse these sounds following: Zeal, Hazard, Raze, wch to write Seal, Hasard, Rase, both otherwise doe sound, and Signify | And now that I am fallen on this matter, pardon my freedome in desiring a little more yor grounds why you pronounce Teth as Th, and Thau as T: contrary to the most Grammarians, And yet much more I wonder at your judgement in the difference of שׂ and שׁ for what yo^w write in the forcecited place Sect: 12, that the Ephraimites jussi dicere Sibboleth dicebant Schibbolet seemes therefore strange because that Schibbolet is of far harder, or more difficult pronunciation the text saith ולא יכין לדבר wch wee render hee could not frame to pronounce it right, wch had been easy if the sound had been Sibbolet, at least to our thinking. But and if the difference lye where I have sometimes conceived it, then the pronunciation were by far more difficult, for of these three sounds ס שׁ and שׂ I have for difference sake conceived these sounds ס as our s in sew as consuere to (sew) שׁ as sh to shew indicare, and שׂ as sch, as to ēschew, vitare, so that every one is a degree dempto ; ē. harder or more difficult then other; to sew, shew, ēschew Job I. 8. there wee use the word and you may here how the English utter it. Herein I crave your judgement as also in ע dicis enim nobis ἀphων [illegible] [Ms. sic], at bene subjungis potius· quam pronunciatio gn : &c. tecum penitus et ego : veruntamen quid obstat, quominus efferatur ut nostrum .y. Consona, cui etiam et figura affinis. uti audies nostrates pronunciantes : Yea, yet, yonder, &c. at diutius in hisce; Cum vero tua scripta summum spirant candorem ; nullus dubito quin æqui, bonique, hæc mea consulas, et quod humillime peto responsum retuleris.

To your 2^{d} We doe not trouble the Indians to Learn ou^{r} English, But onely such as for their own behoof doe it of their owne accord.

To the 3^{d} Mr. Eliot is labouring to bring their tongue under the Skill of Rules of Grammar, and Dictionary, but yo^{w} are mistaken in thinking their Etymologie as single as our English, Albeit this is wonderful in their Tongue that sometimes one Syllable spreads the virtue of its signification through the whole sentence,[1] They are indeed taken greatly in wondering at the skill of the English, and are enforced to confess many times God is among us.

To the 4th they were never offended at o^{r} calling them Indians, as by misinformation, you seem to conceive, but onely inquired of us, the reason of ye name.

To the 5th Wee make what good husbandry wee can of the writing books you sent, but find them of more use to the English, then Indians, being above their capacity, for the present especially being writ in the English Tongue, And herein again I am entreated to render thanks from the severall schooles of the country whereto I have sent them. This answereth also yor 6th and 7th directions.

To yor 8th and 9th The students in the Colledge to whom I have imparted as occasion requireth, yor Hebrew sheet Grammar, wth yor Conjugationall, Hebrew Table doe return you hearty thanks, as I myself doe for yor notes on Udalls Grammar, and yor Orthographicall delineation.

Lastly, wee professe o^{r}selves unable to answer the Tender of your good will and propensity of spirit towards us. Our Infant Colledge compared wth the Academyes in Europe, being like Mantua unto Rome, and as unworthy to confine a man of your parts, and place, as that small Town the Prince of the Latin Poets. Yet neverthelesse if Divine providence should waft you over the Atlantick

[1] In Eliot's Indian Primer, there are words of fifteen syllables. Palfrey.

Ocean, or if yor Spirit desire to see what sons of Seth wander in these woods then Harvard-Colledge would think itselfe honou^rd in yor visit.

Mean time while God's providence continueth you where you bee, as you Tender yor readinesse to further o^r studies, in the Orientall-Tongues, and have already given a reall Testimony of yor benevolent, and beneficent spirit, so if Gods providence put an opportunity into your hand that you help us wth books of those languages from some able hands, and willing hearts (for from yo^rselfe it were unreasonable to expect any more then such books as yo^rselfe are personally the Author of). then should wee bee very glad and evermore thankfull to you, and them, who shall procure us Buxtorfes Concordances ; and Bible (for the King of Spaines we have) and the King of France his Bible is more then wee dare hope for) and whatsoever Hebrew, Caldee, Syriack, or Arabick-authors, Gods providence shall enlarge their hands, and hearts to procure us : A wonderfull impulse unto these studies lyes on the spirits of our students, some of wch can wth ease dextrously translate Hebrew, and Caldee, into Greek. But I forget my selfe in detaining you so long from yor serious, and more profitable Studies : Let mee heare ; I pray, if you received this my letter. The Lord bee wth you, and prosper all yor endeavo^rs. So I Intreat pray for

Yo^rs in the Lord.

Harvard Coll : Cambr : in N E.
Febru : [1648 [1]]

[1] This letter is republished from the Mass. Hist. Coll. IV. Series, I. 251.

VI.

A Copy of Some Part of a Letter written to M[r] Alt, min. of the word of God at Bury in Lancashire.

Reverend and Beloved in the Lord — Lest I sh[d] have no time to write in these my streits of time and stresse of businesse therefore will I take the first time of all Lancashire letters to write yours: heartily thanking you for yours of the 19th of July w[ch] came to hand about the 17th of the 7th [Sept.] by Cozen Mary Dunster, and were very acceptable not onely for the Candor and Piety, that seems to breathe in your Sentences, but also for y[e] matter answering the manner of Style. Controversyes I am unwilling to launch out into; the ocean of Contention overswelling with a spring tyde; insomuch that it overflows the banks of Conscience and drownes the pleasant medows of fruitful love, and all the sweet Pastures of Piety. therefore I can very freely let you abound in your owne Judgment, onely in a word or two to borrow a little light from you what you mean by some of your Expressions.

The gathering of a church scruples you. I pray you S[r] what mean you by Church? the Catholique you cannot mean, National and Provinciall Churches are nullityes in rerum natura since the dissolution of that of the Jewes; I hope you want no light hitherto. Presbyterian? By what rule then are yours gathered or out of what preexistent matter? the Church or the world? If out of the world then you grant that before the Church of England (w[ch] you by M[r] Shepards authority would magnify page

131 Syncere Convert) is not the Church but the world. But this you will never doe. Its a glorious church say you. Whence I pray you was it gathered, out of the Church of Rome or Else yet it stands in it [?] If it stand yet in it, then it is owne of the Daughters of the great whore, pudet haec opprobria nobis, et dici potuisse refelli. Noe, the Church of England is gathered out of Rome — Come out of her my people. Goe to them, Behould a Church gathered out of a Church. True. But its out of the Antichristian Church. Be it. It was Christian apostacy makes it Antichristian; and then if Babilon will not bee healed Depart out of her my people. So (will you say) you Justify England's departure from Rome, and so doth Mr Alt. But why should wee gather a Church out of the English Church? I pray you S^r^, where hath Christ constituted a Church of that form; where's the National ministry Temple &c.: If you wil find this, you have the verity, wee the vanity. If Congregations bee the Visible Churches of Christ wee have the Day in that respect: But say a National Church is a true Church of Christ; Lets see from you by what means wee may doe our duty either to our Brother thats obstinate, or our mother that should rebuke him; Dic Ecclesiae (i.e.) tell ye National Church: who are her ears to hear, her mouth to speak to our Brother that hee may hear. Pape! Papa pater 2^ly^ Bee it; yet suppose this National Church erre and Apostatize fearfully from Christ, profane his Sabbaths, his Sanctuary and ordinances: give holy things to dogs and swine the children's bread, why then come out of her

my people as from Rome, for she also is the image of the beast. Either justify church gathering or disallow our Godly reformers and grandfathers ut Supra. What Mr Shepard said in England (for there were those sermons preached) when he saw no better light must not be laid against his constant practise since, besides his meaning is to bee taken as indeed it was that in England there was a Company of glorious Believers who inwardly & spiritually before Christ are his Church. But I list not to stay to justify any Phrases of men ; That vanity (blessed bee the Lord) is well blasted of humane authority in the Church of Christ, where this Canon is received This is my beloved Sonne hear him, whom the father hath sent to bee head of the Church. To whom who wil not hearken the Lord require it of them Deut. 18, 19: for our part wee are at a poynt in this Isay 33. 22. One word more before I come to ye next Section. I pray you doe you account a single congregation no church then what make you of us all? or rather of the Congregational Churches mentioned in the New Testament? If churches? then How comes Holcom to bee gathered out of Bury or such like, but wth beating to powder your scruples.

Truly S^r^ my Dulnesse cannot frame an answer to these questions I put unto you I hope I shall learn if nothing teach.

To your next Section, you approve the 3d section of ye 3d chapter of our Synod (I need not write out the words. I sent 50 books too you one by this if not before. Let this suffice to them wth whom they bee to give you it) far bee it from me to think you like it because you like corruptions &

would have them patronized: that Section shows no corruptions or Scandals should bee tolerated; but yet they immediately dissolve not &c. No sin but that against the Holy Ghost immediately casts a man to hel. But obstinacy in the least sin casts him gradually out of the Church, if hee hear not his Brother nor Brethren nor the Church. So Dear S^{r} deal with your scandalous ones that know not or obey not ye fayth of Christ, & then your materialls will soon bee right: but I fear few. And then though you gather not a Church out of a Church yet you will throw the world out of ye Church, and have a little gathered flock non congregando but segregando you will have severed a Church from the world, wch is enough. Your instance of the Church of Corinth Sardis &c, you apply not rightly, they were embodied already rightly: and the decayed or corrupt members in them were called on to repentance, least the Lord should lop them off, as hee threatens. John. 15 beg. & had done to many 1 Cor 11. 28 &c, & that Censures might not proceed as Gal. 5:12 & threatens Sardis, Rev. 3. 3. But to speak experimentally if you saw what declining there is in some of the Churches here, & of those very members that had a name to live in Old England & sometime here too, & now what they bee; you would neither need a Comment to know the meaning of that text; nor misse so far the mark, as to take in the world for the Church. When the Churches enjoy peace, though planted generous vines? you shall soon see luxuriant branches of them that for knowledge come to the rule, & for life too for a season. Remember the Parable. Matth. 13. 3. to 24 wch is the Key of all Parables concerning the Kingdome of Heaven, Mark 4. 13. & by wch wee have seen that not onely temporary believers shew their unsound hearts, for fear of persecution for the word, but even those that have tryumpht over persecution, fall by the cares profits or pleasures of the world Luke 8. 14 for persecution hath hardened many in the way for Christ whom the Sunshine hath thawed miserably.

VII.

Part of a Letter to some Christian friends in and about Bury in Lancashire.

Sundry reasons move mee at this time to shut you all up in one letter in all whose sundry letters I find the same spirit breathing, ye same gratious desires (though for manner diversified some little yet for their matter the same viz: that God would guide you by his light and truth in his ways of holiness & peace. Yet truly all your letters speak such plain & candid expressions of your single sincere hearts, that for my part I can wth every good assurance in my owne heart believe Christ Jesus hath gathered you all in one & the same Church mysticall & spirituall even into that body whereof hee is the head, in whom if you lovingly strive together in fayth and love, then for outward administrations bear kindly one with another where you cannot by the word of ye Lord clearly convince your Brother of sinne. I have seen with much shame of face much folly & sin & in swelling words & bitter Invectives against persons or things where clearnes of reason and evidence of God's word is wanting to bee matter of conviction to their spirits, against whom such words have been darted. It's not a painted flame though never so lively, that consumeth stubble and fuel, but real material fire will doe it. If any that utter big & bitter Invectives against the congregationall way can convince any members of ye same that they have separated themselves from the saynts & people of God that they may live profanely, unrighteously, luxuriantly and wantonly &c or to any other end that is contrary to sound Doctrine I think they shall doe welle to admonish them by ye word of the Lord which they have transgresst. But if they onely have withdrawn themselves from communion of & communicating with the Dark, prophane & scandalous world that lyeth in that evill one 1 Jo: 5. 19. that knoweth not Christ nor hath receyved his spirit that they may live together in holy communion with Christ and his people in all his instituted ordinances, Then I say whosoever condemn these people, Christ his word will justify them to & before all his true Churches in ye world. And his spirit will speak peace to their spirits whoever have so done in sincerity, as unto Sonnes & Daughters of the living God. Glorious I confesse and forever Honourable to those Instruments of Christ is that passage in the 33d page of the Vindication of the Armies declaration against the Scots' reply. Give us leave to aske you of Scotland, who alone would seeme to be the true Reformers, whether wee have any nationall sins, as the compulsive Joyning of the pretious with the vile in the administration of the seales of the Covenant of grace, or the corrupt & horrible Constitution of the matter of your Churches, making them up of people grossly ignorant & very scandalous &c.

If King Charles with the house of Lords & Commons had breathed such a principle of reforming verily, by way of Edict, proclamation or Statute that ye saints should forbear themselves & the prophane world by no means compeld to church communion, All the chief priests & elders & doctors would have cryed out Hosannah, & Ador'd him with as much admiration as the Jews would their Messias if he had come in such worldly pomp & grandeur as they fancied. But if ye Lord Jesus come in his owne way here in the kingdom of grace, in poor, low popular[1] men and means like a refiners fyer & fullers soap, purifying the Sonns of Levi, a swift witness against all prophaneness and Ignorance, witches, adulterers, swearers, &c Mal. 3: Then who may abide ye day of his coming? it's Darkness & not light to many souls Amos 5. 18. We would either have a Christe come for manner after our fancies, or else we will reject him, though he come full of Grace and Truth, that wee may see him, even his glory, ye glory of ye only begotten of the father, not in his physicall person only, but in measure stampt on his Ordinances, on his servants, on his marvelous works that he doth for his people, whereoff no nation under heaven hath larger experience (if their eyes were open to see it) than now ye English nation, for whom, And specially for

[1] i.e., common, inferior.

their Godly Parliament and Victorious Army, we fast & pray. We also feast & rejoice, & see much, yea very much of ye Lord Jesus Christ with them & amongst them ; And purpose on ye 10th of January in all ye churches in & about ye Bay publickly to rejoice before the Lord for all ye wonderfull works of ye Lord done for his churches & people in England, Ireland & Scotland, from ye beginning, but specially this last summer unto ye 20th of 7^ber^ [September] whithertoo our Intelligence by ye last ship (Capt. Gookins) reacheth. This I ye rather write, becaus you desire to know how the churches here relish the proceedings with you. Truely wee are all one heart[1] (I mean ye body of ye Godly) with ye parliament & Army, And see that Christ hath carried them beyond men & themselves in all they have (not so much chosen to do, as) by his impulse in a sort been driven to doe. If

[1] There were at least two decided exceptions, in Rev. James Noyes and Rev. Thomas Parker, of Newbury, who were staunch royalists. The latter writing of the former, says, "Upon the rising of our late Usurpers [Cromwell] and the beheading of our late gracious and most excellent King Charles the first, of blessed memory, by a villanous stroke, and under a wicked pretence of Justice, and upon the defeating of our renowned King Charles the second (whom God preserve), he fell into such a depth of sadnesse and sorrow of heart, that it hastened his death, as was believed." In the "Epistle Dedicatory to the King" (Charles II.), he further says, "The report of proclaiming your Majesty and your most joyful return into England hath wrought in our hearts incredible joy and gladnesse. And I am like the servant of Elias looking out, & looking seven times, till I see the little cloud arising that shall increase more & more, till all the heavens be covered with clouds, & a great rain of righteousness come down upon the earth to refresh the hearts of men parched with drought."

they had ever found Charles pliable to termes of piety & righteousness in sincerity, & not still doubling with them, he had been King unto this day. But whoever eyther reads Mayes[1] story, or Heeds ye Kings words & Declarations with his contradictory Actions, shall be forced (yea though he weer ye Kings owne sonne to say he deserted to Scotland [?][2] by ye Lord's appointment, Proverbs 28, 17, wee wonder that Scotland would force young Charles the fathers owne sonne to condemn old Charles his own very father as justly demeriting all that hath befaln him & his house, from God & his Instrument ye state of England,[3] & yet when they have done quarrell

[1] The History of the Parliament of England, which began Nov. 3, 1640. By Thomas May, 1649.

[2] The ms. is here obscure, but the probable reading is that given in the text. The reference seems to be to the time when Charles, in consequence of severe disasters, resolved to throw himself into the hands of the Scottish Army.

[3] After the establishment of the Commonwealth, Charles II., who had been a refugee, came to Scotland, at the invitation of the Scots, who proclaimed him their king. He was crowned on New Year's Day [March] 1651; when he hypocritically submitted to the humiliation of swearing "that he would prosecute the ends prescribed in the Covenant, and agree to all acts of Parliament for the establishment, in his Scotch realms, of Presbyterian rule, of the Directory, and the Confession and Catechism of the Kirk." He was also "reminded how his grandfather James had broken his vow, and been plagued therefor, and was forced into a confession of his father's sin in marrying an idolatress, and to declare his resolution to do nothing but with the advice of the Kirk."—Stoughton, Church of the Commonwealth, ii. 39.

This historical reference fixes the date of the letter as late probably as 1652. It also proves that Mr. Dunster's rejection of infant baptism was after this date; which agrees with the year (1653), mentioned by Cotton Mather, when he preached against that practice. See p. 109 of this work, and note 1.

with England for doing such an act of glorious justice that is so clear that not only unbiassed minds but even a mans natural son must see by its light else he is worthy to be cast out of Kirk.

And why the good people of England should not own (at least to be faithfull unto) ye present State Constitution, I confess I neither have heard, seen, nor can gather any sound reason. For ye monarchy: Man's wickedness as ye meritorious Cause, and God's Providence and mighty hand as ye efficient Cause hath dissolved [it]. The nation then is free from it Rom. 7, 1. &c by proportion [?]. No man's oth tyeth him to what is not. If the people and nation be free from monarchy, ye question is what form they should set up? And what I pray you but that which is most sutable to ye Matter? I say, to ye form which is most suitable to ye Matter, which the nation itself by their faithfull representatives, being pious & prudent men, can best judge off. As in spiritualls so in temporalls, God would fain doe us good, but we will not accept it. How true is all ye 26. I say verify'd of the English nation spiritually 10, 11 &c. [?] But I hope ye Lord for his own glorious Name sake [will] perfect the work to his own prayse, that hitherto he hath so gloriously promoted. For ye lifted up hand of ye Lord hath effected Terrible things in righteousness, and answering prayers hetherto in England, Wales, Ireland & Scotland. And I pray him to give you wisdom to see it; And to fill you with ye spirit of holiness and reall reformation which is now breathed into, & breathes in some of the chief persons that manage ye affairs

Civill and Politicall in parliament and Army. And this you may quietly doe off and amongst yourselves by the directory of God's Word, Least if nothing will content our countrymen But a reformation of ye Scottish edition, It leav you in deep distress inward [and] outward. If not in [ ]. I must Contract, for truely my time is out, & other weighty businesses call on me. To answer you briefly some of your questions, positively not polemically, by dissolving all objections. 1st Is it lawfull to separate from one Congregation or gather a church out of them?

1 Answer If your Congregation at Bury bee a Church of Christ, & not lawfull to gather a Church out of them, how come Holcom Lawfully a Church distinct from yours? How shall any church that is too numerous to meet in one place (as Boston in New England) lawfully permit their members to constitute a second[1] in their towne or villages, who can doubt of this?

2dly If a company of men Cohabiting become a Congregation, which, be it right or wrong, were at first gathered into a Church, & by Long Tract of time have lost all sense and power of religion, & take Gods name in vain by a prophane abuse of his Ordinance: Now, when a day of love light & grace comes, will forsake the evill of their former ways, & do hold out, every one as he is called, that he receiveth ye truth, reforms his way, brings forth fruit worthy of repentance: so many as thus doe, call'd together, are to renew their Covenant & to own

[1] This fixes the date of this letter as late at least as 1650 or 1651, as the Second Church of Boston was gathered on the 5th day of June, 1650.

ye Lord God of their fathers: & walking in all his will as it's manifested to them, such so doing become visible saints, & a Church of Christ's for what I see. But ye rest, that seclude themselves by their visible profaneness, separate themselves from the Church, 2 Cro. 30. 10. Accept of all that understandingly owne ye doctrine & Discipline of Christ; & leav them or let them alone that know him not their priest that hath made their atonement with ye father; that hear him not as their prophet, Deut. 18. 19, that own him not their king, to be subject to plain and undisputable Rules of his will. Then will you soon find ye world will leav ye Church.

2 Q. If the Churches or Congregations of England were ever by that voyse of Christ, Come out of her my people, gathered from ye Romish apostacy?

Ans. Judge yourselves if ye sword of ye Spirit, or that of ye Civill Magistrate from Hen[ry] 8 his time [to] yours have severed the English from the Romish Church. Yet I will confess the Sword of [the] Spirit hath gathered Sundry Souls home to Christ, as [to] day, blessed be ye Lord, it doth sundry Indians with us.

2 Q. What sufficient matter of cutting off Members from ye Churches?

Ans. All scandalous sins, such as 1 Cor. 5: 11 &c.

2^d. All sins Against any clear rule that a man obstinately will hold. If obstinacy after conviction appear in idle words, he is not a visible subject of Christ.

4 Q. What do you with them that are baptized, but give no satisfactory testimony of piety when they come to age, And what with their children?

Ans. None of their children are baptized untill one of ye parents at ye least do approve themselves faithfull & be joyned to ye Church. I have herewith sent you Mr. Davenport's Catechism, where ye question is handled, & answered according to practice. As for such persons themselves, such there be amongst us with whom ye Church bears patiently, using means for their Conviction & Conversion. And in case they break out into any unchristain courses, admonish them, & if they continue in them, wholy withdraw from them. But I have not knowne any of these formally excommunicated because they neither cared for nor sought Communion.

5 Q. What do you in Case divers bewray unsoundness in ye Churches? and yet not faulty enough to be excommunicated?

Ans. Some deserve excommunication, of whose sincerity in the main we have no Cause to doubt. It's therefore an ordinance of Christ to bring home a soul far and fouly straying.

2^ly^ Those that are not lyable to excommunication, because their sin is neither of a Heynous Nature, nor yet they obstinate therein, & to be admonished and restored with a spirit of Love. And if this amend them not (for so you write) then are they either dead, fruitless branches, not sencible, not indeed truly capable of Christ's ordinances, as Civill Worldlings: or if knowing & possessors, they are obstinate & to be cast out.

VIII.

CONFERENCE AT BOSTON.

H. D[unster] cum seni. Mr. Wilson, Norton, Mather, Thomson, Allen, Eliot, Sims, Danforth, Mitchell, Colebon, Pen.

Feb. 2, 1653–4.

Thesis — Soli visibiliter fideles sunt baptizandi. H. D[unster.]

[Visible believers only should be baptized.]

Mr. Jo[hn] N[orton].— We grant it, but say infants of believing parents in church state are visible believers.

Mr. D[unster].— Neg[at].

Mr. N[orton].— Prob[at]. If infants of believers under the Gospel be as capable of being visible believers as y[e] infants of believers under y[e] Law, unto whom y[e] original promise was made, then infants under the gospel are visible believers. At ergo.

Mr. D[unster].— Neg. Maj.

Mr. N[orton].— There can no reason be given why infants under the law should be visible believers more than infants now. Ergo.

Mr. D[unster].— This reason may be given, because God made a special promise to Abraham concerning his seed.

Mr. N[orton].— If the visibility of believers depend on divine testimony, there be as much now as then. Then it follows, at ergo. All Abraham's seed were visible believers.

Mr. D[unster].— neg :

Mr. N[orton].— prob : All that were circumcised were visible believers ; but all were circumcised. Maj : prob : Circumcision was a testimony of their visible faith. Ergo, Rom. 4 : 11. If the child that was circumcised & did not believe was guilty of breach of covenant in not believing, then infants in circumcision did profess to believe. At Ergo.

Mr. D[unster].— neg. Min : if infants die unbelievers in infancy were guilty of breach of covenant.

Mr. N[orton].— Either infants dying in infancy in unbelief were not guilty of violation of the covenant, or else they were guilty in not believing. But they were guilty of the violation of the covenant if they died in infancy in unbelief. Ergo.

Mr. D[unster].— Infants have no illicit act of faith.

Mr. N[orton].— Actuall faith is one thing, actuall [active ?] faith is another. Christ in infansie & a man asleep have actuall faith, but do not actively believe.

That infants have faith. 1. If Adam had stood, his children should have been born with original righteousness of God, with faith in God, i. e. ye faith proper to that covenant. 2. Christ as infant had faith as the covenant was made Ct. 3. Divine test: concerning children that God is their God, Acts 2 : 38, 39 whence to us.

Those to whom ye promise of remission of sin, according to ye sense of Acts 2 : 38 are visible saints. But infants under the gospel are such to whom ye promise of remission of sins is made &c.

Mr.D[*unster*].— It is offered.

Mr. N [*orton*].— It is a remission really given to them in Col. 2 : 11, 12.

Mr. S [*imms*].— Either Paul there speaks of external completeness without reference to children, or else he doth not there prove that children are as complete in external privileges under ye Gospel as under ye Law.

Mr. D[*unster*].— He doth not meddle with children.

Mr. S [*imms*].— Ans. If he speaks of ye saints' completeness in regard of externall privileges, then of children. If about children was part of ye objection of false teachers, then ye Apostle in his answer about ye completeness speaks of children, At ergo.

Mr. N[*orton*].— If ye false teachers' objection was, according to ye law of Moses, grounded on Mosaicall rites, then it was about children, for ye false teachers urging circumcision speak of children.

Mr. D[*unster*].— Children under ye gospel have Christ's express testimony that they have a nearer access unto him, & a nearer acceptance with him, than children under ye Law, viz. in Matt. 19: & Mark 10:, in that when John Baptist, Christ himself & Apostles did none of them baptize children, Christ to support ye spirit of parents gave yet more express testimony than we remember to be under ye law, concerning his good will to their children in respect of that best and nearest acceptance with him, viz. their eternal salvation.

Dic : Feb. 3*d. Mr. A*[*llen*]. *Moderat.*

Quest : Whether baptisme of any infants be a Gospel institution ?

Mr. M[*ather*].— Affir : Baptisme of all their members is a Gospel Institut : But baptisme of some infants is Baptisme of Cch : mem^{brs}.

Mr. D[*unster*].— Neg : et Maj. et Min : For all church members are not to be baptised, as ye Jews at John's preaching.

Mr. M.[1]— All ye members of ye Cch : of ye N. T. are to be baptised. At ergo, But some Infants are memb^{rs} of ye church of ye N. T. go.

Major prob : That which was one end why C[hris]t gave himself, that ought to be attended. But yet all ye M^{brs} of ye Church of ye N.T. should be baptised, for ye Baptisme of all ye M.^{brs} of ye Ch[urch] of ye N.T. was an end why C[hris]t gave himselfe.

Mr. D[*unster*]. — Neg : Min :

Mr. M. — prob : by the express word of Eph. 5. He gave himselfe for his Ch[urch] that he might sanctify it by ye washing of water — by water is meant baptisme. Now if baptisme be ye constituted means to ye end of sanctifying ye Ch[urch], what was ye end for which C[hris]t gave himself [other] than baptisme ? At ergo.

Mr. D[*unster*]. — Ans : Means whether instituted or prudential are to accomplish ye end, but they are not ye end for which C[hris]t died, for so afflictions & fals of

[1] More likely Mr. Mather than Mr. Mitchell, the latter being a much younger man.

ye Saints are used by C[hris]t for ye sanctifying of ye Ch[urch], but yet we say not that C[hris]t gave hims : that ye saints might have afflictions and fals.

Ans. *Mr. N[orton]*. — The lapse & fall of a s[ain]t was not in itselfe a means, but the sanctifying of ye lapse, now this he gave himselfe for.

Argument. That which is by right as largely applyable (or equally extended by) sanctification, that is applyable to ye whole Ch[urch], or to all ch: M^brs^. But Ephes. 5, Baptisme or washing of water is by right (or lawful instituted use) as largely applyable as sanctification. Ergo, it is applicable to all Ch. Memb^rs^.

Againe to the first Major.

Mr. M. — The body of C[hrist] may be baptised. All memb^rs^ of ye Ch : of ye N.T. (taken joyntly together) are ye Body of C[hris]t, gô. or thus, All that are Me[m]b^rs^ of ye Body of C[hris]t may be baptised. But all Ch: M[em]b^rs^ of the N.T. are M[em]b^rs^ of ye body of C[hris]t. ergo.

Mr. D[unster]. — Take ye M[em]b^rs^ of Christ's body in [the] largest sense Neg : Major.

Mr. M. — 1 Cor. 12 : 12, 13.

Mr. D[unster]. — All that were baptised were baptised into ye Body, but all y^t^ [that] are of the body are not to be baptised.

Mr. M. — If Baptisme be ye Means to seal up their incorporation into that Body of C[hris]t, then all that are of that Body may lawfully be baptised. At, gô.

Againe, how can all ye M[em]b^rs^ make one body, if Baptisme be not belonging to all ye Memb^rs^ of that body, as vs 12. If ye Apost. bring this Argum[en]t of baptising into one body to prove that all ye M[em]brs are one body, then baptisme belongs (it is Extendable) to all ye M[em]brs of that Body. At ergo.

Ans. 1 Cor. 10. The L[or]ds Supp[er] seals ye unity of all into one body, & yet all that are of ye body may not p[ar]take of ye Supp[er].

Min: of first Syllogisme. If Infants were sometimes Membrs of ye Ch[urch], & their membership was under repeale, then some infants are M[em]brs of ye Ch[urch] of ye N.T. At, ergo.

Mr. D[unster]. — Negat Minor:

Mr. M. — prob. If ye M[em]bership of Infants be repealed, it is either in Mercy for their good or in judgment to their hurt. But neither of these. Ergo.

Mr. D[unster]. — Ans. We are not to dive into God's ends for repealing it. It sufficeth us that the Lord hath repealed it — Or it is repealed in mercy to ye elect infants, in judgment to ye vessels of wrath.

Mr. M. — Not in mercy for their good. If it be repealed in mercy for their good, either it was before for their hurt, or elsę there is some other good given them in lue of it. But neither of these — Ergo, That no good is given. If no good besides membership be given to infants now but what they had before, then there is no good given them in lue of their M[em]bership. At, gô.

[*Dunster*]. — Neg: Minor:

[*M*]. — prob. If besides M[em]bership, they have all their internall & externall priviledges before that now they have, then there is no good given them besides M[em]-bership that they had not before. At, gô.

Min : prob : That the same covenant & the blessings of it heretofore, viz. under the Law, *that* they have now, then they had the same priviledges internall and externall that now they have.

Againe they of old besides M[em]bership had all the species though not gradus [degree] of any good that besides m[em]bership now they can have, but takeing away of m[em]bership, a Gradus of yᵉ former good will not Answer or be in lue of that Species.

Mr. M. — Arg : If it be simply a judgment for any one to be out of yᵉ visible politicall Ch[urch], Then infants are not now taken out of yᵉ Ch[urch] in mercy. At : gô.

Mr. D[unster]. — Neg. Min : That which God hath appointed for a punishment of sin, that is simply to any one a judgm[e]nt, but to be taken out of yᵉ Ch[urch] God hath appointed to be a punishment of sin. ergo. Or, to be out of visible relation to good is simply a judgm[e]nt. But to be out of the visible Ch[urch] is to be out of a visible Relation to God.

Mr. D. — Neg. Min.

Mr. M. — Prob : Min. If when the Ephesians, 2. 11, were out of a visible political Church they were without God in the world, then to be out of a visible political Church is to be out of a visible relation to God. gô.

Mr. D[unster] — Neg. Min. For they were when called in yᵉ Catholique Ch[urch].

Mr. M. — If they were Aliens from the Commonwealth

of Israel &c. then without. But when they were out of a visible politicall Ch[urch] they were Aliens &c.

Mr. D[unster]. — Neg. Min.

Mr. M. — To be out of yᵉ Commonwealth of Israel is to be without God in yᵉ world. But to be out of yᵉ visible political Church is to be out of yᵉ Commonwealth of Israel Ergo.

Mr. D[unster]. — Neg. Min.

Mr. Wils[on] — To be out of yᵉ Arke is a judgm[e]nt. But to be out yᵉ visible Ch[urch] is to be out of yᵉ Arke. ergo.

Mr. D[unsier]. — Neg. Min.

Mr. M. — Againe, To be visibly under yᵉ power of Satan is a judgm[e]nt. But to be out of yᵉ visible politicall Ch[urch] is to be under yᵉ power of Satan.

Mr. D[unster]. — Neg. Min.

Mr. M. — If to be cast out of yᵉ Ch[urch] is to be delivered or put under yᵉ visible power of Satan, then to be out of yᵉ Ch[urch] is to be visibly under yᵉ power of Satan, at. Ergo.

Mr. D[unster]. — Neg : Cons[eq.] Maj.

Mr. M. — If Satan doe visibly reigne out of yᵉ visible politicall ch[urch], Then to be cast out of yᵉ visible ch[urch] is to be visibly under yᵉ power of Satan. At. ergo.

Mr. D[unster]. — Neg. Min.

Mr. M. — Where Satan is visibly a God there he reignes. But out of yᵉ visible politicall Ch[urch] Satan is visibly a God. Ergo.

Mr. D[*unster*]. — Min. not true of all persons out of y[e] visible politicall Ch[urch].

Mr. A[*llin*]. — To want the visible Government of C[hris]t is simply a judgm[e]nt. But to be out of y[e] visible politicall ch[urch] is to want y[e] visible government of Christ. Ergo.

Mr. N[*orton*]. — To make the comming of C[hris]t a judgm[e]nt unto Infants is an error. But to make infants M[em]bership repealed by y[e] comming of C[hris]t in the Flesh, is to make the comming of C[hris]t a judgm[e]nt unto Infants, [er]go. That Tenent [tenet] which makes the coming of Christ a judgm[e]nt to elect infants is unsound. But to deny pedobaptisme makes the coming of Christ to be in judgm[e]nt to elect Infants, ergo.

Mr. D[*unster*]. — Neg. Min.

Mr. N[*orton*]. — That it deprives infants of y[e] seals of the Covenant, makes y[e] coming of C[hris]t in judgm[e]nt. But to deny pedobaptism upon y[e] coming of C[hris]t deprives Infants of y[e] seals of y[e] covenant. Ergo.

Mr. D[*unster*]. — Neg. Min. It does not deprive them.

Mr. N[*orton*]. — If infants before y[e] coming of C[hris]t had y[e] seals which now they have not, it deprives them. Or, If y[e] coming of C[hris]t takes away from infants that seal of y[e] coven[an]t which before they had then it deprives them. At. ergo.

Mr. D[*unster*]. — Its a negation, not a privation, for y[e] seal is out of date, and y[e] other not instituted to Infants.

Mr. N[*orton*]. — If it be a taking away of a good which y[e] subject was possessed of before, then it's a privation, not a Negation only. Or, If to be in a capacity or to be made p[ar]taker of ye seal of ye covenant of grace be a good [—] if this which they had before is now taken away from them then it is a taking away of a good which they were before possessed of. At. ergo.

Mr. D[unster]. — Neg. Maj. If or though C[hris]t take away that capacity of or right to ye seal, yet he gives them something else which is better.

Mr. N[orton]. — If C[hris]t by his coming takes away both seal, coven[an]t and present right to a seal, and doth not either give them any equivalent ordinance, or any present right to any such ordinance, then he brings in a personal privation of Good, without making it up with anything else. At. [er]go.

Mr. N[orton]. — Arg: That opinion that leaves Infants less holy under ye gospel than under ye Mosaicall dispensation is not sound. But ye opinion that denies children ch[urch] membership (or pedobaptisme) so doth — ergo.

Mr. D[unster]. — Neg. Min.

Mr. N[orton]. — Prob. They were then holy to ye holiness of ye participation of ye seal of ye coven[an]t, and then holy to ye holyness of Ch[urch] M[em]bership. But this they have not now. Ergo.

Mr. D[unster]. — Ans. They had it by institution then, as also to eat ye passover as soon as they could eat meat in ye family, therefore ye Argument from such Analogy is not conclusive.

Mr. N[orton]. — It cannot be prooved that any might eat of ye passover who (in regard of their discretion to discern) might not be capable of eating ye Lord's supper.

Againe They only that could discern y[e] doctrine of the passover might eat y[e] passover, and they also that can discern y[e] Doctrine of y[e] L[or]d's supp[er] may eate it.

H[ENRY] D[UNSTER] OPPONENT.

1 Arg. All instituted Gospel worship hath some expresse word of Scripture. But pedobaptisme hath none. Ergo.

Mr. N[*orton*]. — It hath a word by manifest consequence.

Mr. D[*unster*]. — Then that's in either y[e] old Test[ament] or N[ew] ; but neither.

Mr. N[*orton*]. — In both. But prove it's not in y[e] N[ew].

Mr. D[*unster*]. — If in y[e] N[ew], either it's in Johns baptisme, or Christ's or his Disciples.

Mr. N[*orton*]. — In Johns, though not only.

Mr. D[*unster*]. — If John only baptised penitent believers confessing their sins. Then not infants. At. ergo.

Mr. N[*orton*]. — Neg. Maj.

Mr. D[*unster*]. — They that cannot speak are not penitent believers confessing their sins. At. ergo.

Mr. N[*orton*]. — They speak virtually, i.e. as they that were circumcised acknowledging y[e] coven[an]t sealed to which implyes confession of sins. We all in Adam did virtually speak a word in y[e] coven[an]t of works.

Mr. D[*anforth*]. — Soe may we be baptised in our parents.

Mr. D[*unster*]. — If we be engrafted into C[hris]t by personall faith, then not by parentall. At. ergo.

Mr. N[*orton*]. — Conceditur [granted]. but an infant makes his covenant in his publique p[er]son.

Mr. D[*unster*]. — There is now noe publique person but C[hris]t for us to stand in.

Mr. N[*orton*]. — An immediate parent is a publique p[er]son in regard of his children yea in respect to a covenant bought with Money as an Indian child, that in his Infansie doth devenire in potestatem ejus,[1] and is his to have plenary power over him, as Abraham's servants. I say, such a one may be baptised.

Mr. D[*anforth*]. — What say you to that holynesse mentioned 1 Cor. 7. 14?

Mr. D[*unster*]. — The holinesse there is not meant of federall holinesse only of ye children of ch[urch] M[em]-bers, for if soe then none that are out of ye church have such holy children, But some that [are] out of the politicall church have such holy children.

Mr. N[*orton*]. — Neither have they soe.

Mr. D[*unster*]. — Every true believer though not of ye ch[urch] hath such holy children.

Mr. N[*orton*]. — Holinesse there as in Rom. 11. 16. and Malachy is spoken only of p[er]sons in ch[urch] estate.

Mr. W[*ilson*]. — The woman of Caanan was a true believer and yet she and her children were dogs.

Omnes Q. — But what say you to the place?

Mr. D[*unster*]. — Holinesse in the 1 Cor. 17 is expounded, and by most expositors, as Ambrose &c, of the legitimate issue from God's holy institution of marriage.

[1] Devenire ad aliquem in servitutem. Plautus.

So Musculus, Camer[arius]. 2. Of Designation to God's service, and holy education by C[hris]tian parents, as Tertullian et caeteri. 3 Of federation, as most Calvinists. 4. Of Mutuall holy use, commerce and conversation.

Mr. N[orton]. — 1. Children of infidels are legitimate.

2. Noe General designation to the service of God but by cov[ena]nt or federation. 3. Unclean, i.e. common, is opposite to cov[ena]nt holynesse.

Mr. D[unster]. — If the ch[ildre]n of believers be holy by such a separating federall holynesse, then they are as the Jews of old separated by a wall of separation from the ch[ildre]n of unbelievers, or of the world.

Mr. N[orton]. — The wall of separation is the wall of ceremoniall uncleannesse by the Mosaicall rites, whereby the Gentiles were farre off. But there is a separating difference between the children of the ch[urch] and others, under the N[ew] T[estament]. . . .

IX.

"Rev. John Clarke, . . . Obadiah Holmes, . . . and John Crandall were deputed by the [Newport] Church to visit an aged member, [William Witter] residing near Lynn, who had requested an interview with some of his brethren. Arriving at the place on Saturday, Mr. Clarke preached the next day to those who were in the house. While thus engaged, two constables served on them a warrant for the arrest of the 'erroneous persons, being strangers.' In the afternoon they were carried to church by the officer, where, after service, Clarke addressed the congregation till silenced by a magistrate. Next day, although being under arrest, he administered the communion to the aged member of his church and to two others. The party were examined, and ordered to be sent to Boston, where they were imprisoned to await their trial the following week. At the trial Gov. Endicott charged them with being anabaptists. Clarke denied that he was either an anabapatist, a pedobaptist, or a catabaptist, and affirmed, that although he had baptised many he had never re-baptised any, for that infant baptism was a nullity. The others agreed in this, and the Court sentenced them upon their own declarations, 'without producing either accuser, witness, jury, law of God or man.' Clarke was fined twenty-five pounds, Holmes thirty pounds, and Crandall five pounds, and in default of payment each was 'to be well whipped.' They refused to pay the fine, as that would be to admit their guilt when they felt they were innocent, and were committed to prison. On the following day Clarke, by a letter to the Court, challenged the members to a discussion of the doctrinal views for which he had been condemned. The magistrates appointed a time for the debate. Clarke prepared the heads of discussion, but before the day arrived an order of Court was sent to the jail for his discharge, the fine having been paid by some one without his knowledge. Anxious to hold the debate, and seeing how this ill-timed kindness might be represented as being caused by his desire to avoid it, Clarke, on the same day, renewed the challenge, offering to come to Boston at any time they might name. In their reply, the Court seemed to accept the invitation, but fixed no time. Cotton was to be the chosen champion of Puritan theology — the man of all others . . . with whom Clarke most desired to meet, and to discuss the two great principles of Baptist faith, voluntary baptism and individual responsibility . . . But although Clarke a third time notified the Court of his readiness, they failed to appoint a day, so that the debate was never held. Crandall was allowed to go home on bail, the jailer being his surety. Holmes was so cruelly whipped, receiving thirty lashes with a three-corded whip from the public executioner, that for many days he could take no rest, except by supporting himself on his elbows and knees. Two of the spectators, one an old man named Hazel, who had come from Seekonk, fifty miles, to visit him in prison, were arrested for shaking hands with him after the punishment was over, and were sentenced to pay a fine or to be whipped. The fine was paid by their friends, but Hazel died before reaching home." History of the State of Rhode Island, by S. G. Arnold, I. pp. 234, 235. See also "Ill Newes from New England," by John Clarke.

X.

MR. DUNSTER'S WILL.

"O Lord, my times are in thy hands, and I fully submitt unto thine appoyntments, for my dissolution committinge my spirit in to thy hands for thou hast redeemed it, and hast by manifold deliverances out of Tribulation sealed to my soule the truth of thy word concerninge thy fatherly love and care of me, but especially by thine own secret and cleare spirit of grace sealing to my heart that which noe mortall understanding or spiritt could possibly conceive without God — wherefore, committing both soul and body in life and death and resurrection unto thee, and my poore family after my decease, to whom thou wilt be a father and protector; as I hope now to procure peace as much as in me lyeth concerninge these earthly goods of which thou hast made me steward, I order and constitute this my last will and testament in manner and forme followinge.

Imprimis, my will and testament is, that after moderate funerall expenses discharged, wherein I include that if God's providence by winds and tide do sute, twenty shillings shall be Allowed to any that shall transport my body to Charlestowne — or if to Cambridge thirty shillings, and five shillings apiece to eight bearers that shall carry it from Charlestowne to Cambridge there to be enterred by my loveing wife and other relac̃c̃ons. After my funerall expenses discharged, then my will is, that of all my lands and houses, household goods and all manner of debts, dues and rights to me appertaininge, whether in present action or by annuall bonds emergent, as in the case of Edmund Rice, the same my will is that there be taken a true and just inventory thereof so farre as man's wisdom can Attaine. But whereas the value of my Library cannot bee taken but by judicious and learned men som of my bookes beinge in such languages wherein common English men know not one letter, therefore I do appoint my reverend and trusty friends and brethren, the President of the Colledge, and the pastor of the Church of Cambridge, both to vallue them and lay asside the bookes hereafter specifyed as given to my wife, viz. The book of Martirs in two vollumes, Dr. Preston's workes, Mr. Burroughs' workes, All bookes of Phisicke and surgery that are in the English tongue, with twelve or sixteen bookes brought by her out of England, wherein I will have her word for a legall testimony, because it is good and vallid unto mee in my will. The other two moyties of my library, I with the consent of my wife have by deed and gift given and bequeathed unto my two sons David and Jonathan Dunster, to be equally divided between them, and to be delivered unto them as they shall have need of any particular books, and the whole bulke of them when they come to maturity of age. And after all cleare debts honestly discharged, that then my other goods be equally divided into three equal parts, whereof retayninge one third part to my selfe in legacies to be bequeathed as I see meet, a second part my will is, that my wife shall choose, and the other third part to be bestowed upon my three children equally according to the discretion of my executors. As for my lands, my will is, that my wife shall have the third of the rent of all my lands during her life. But I constitute and appoynt David and Jonathan Dunster Heyres to the said land, divided into two just equal divisions, and whereas the law of Massachusetts[1] requires the Eldest brother to be indowed with a double portion, Thereunto I answer, that I have given unto my son David liberall education in schools of learning from his childhood unto this very day, and the Lord continuing my life, I shall continue the said fatherly care of him, wherefore if hee thinks that considing this, he hath hard measure to have but only equall with his brother, then let him cause that in Godly schooles of literature his brother Jonathan to be brought up in the knowledge of the lattine and principles of the greeke Tongue untill hee come to the age that my son David shall be at my decease, this being performed, he shall have a double porc̃c̃on of lands and goods, otherwise I take it I have fulfilled the law in the letter thereof. Concerning my daughter Elisabeth,[2] my mind and will is, that she shall be at the disposing of her mother during her life in her minority, and in the case of my wive's death, then to live with my sister Mrs. Hills[3] of Mauldon during her

[1] Body of Liberties, Art. 81.

[2] Born in 1656.

[3] "The sisters of the President were Elisabeth and Mary, who successively were wives of Major Simon Willard; the latter survived him and married Dea. Joseph Noyes, of Sudbury, and a third, perhaps Rose, was wife of Captain Joseph Hills, of Malden." Savage. Gen. Dict. II. 82. Elisabeth died childless. Mary was the one alluded to in the will.

It has been made a question, however, whether Mary was a sister or cousin of the President. Willard (Memoir, 351) suggests that if she was a cousin, she might, perhaps, as the wife of a brother-in-law, be called sister. A letter of Mr. Dunster's to Rev. Mr. Alt, of Bury, Eng., contained in the "Dunster Papers," in the possession of the Mass. Hist. Society, speaks of his "cosin Mary Dunster." But there is no proof that she became the wife of Major Willard. There may still have been a sister named Mary, which seems altogether the most probable inference from the decided language of the will.

minority, and faithfully and carefully to serve her as if shee were her own child, and in case there also the Lord by death should make such uncomfortable breaches in the family, that shee could not live comfortably there, then shee shall live with my sister Willard of Concord doing her faythfull service as a child untill her marriage or maturity of age, at which time I do appoynt her to receive from her two brothers, David and Jonathan, five pounds apiece, annually for ten years space, beside what legacys her mother or my selfe shall leave her. Concerning the third part, I reserved in my own hands, I thus dispose thereof as followeth. Item. I give and bequeath unto Mr. Chauncy[1] such mathematicke bookes as hitherto I have lent him, with what household goods I left at Cambridge, viz. my great press in the Hall chamber and another press for bookes in the Study. Item, I give and bequeath unto Mr. Michell[2] Rollocke's Commentaries upon John, which heretofore I lent him, with all the rest of that holy man's Commentaries upon the Scriptures that shall be found in my library, that himself hath not already. Item. I give and bequeath to the holy servant of the Lord Elder ffrost Twenty shillings, and to my cousin Bowers and her children five shillings apeece, and to my cousin fayth Dunster five shillings, and to my sister Willard and all her children five shillings apeece, and to my sister Hills and all her children Borne in this country five shillings apeece, and my will is that my faythfull Mayd Mary Russell should have 15 shillings added to her wages. What then shall

[1] President Chauncy. [2] Rev. Jonathan Mitchell, of Cambridge.

remain of this third part, my will is that my wife shall have a third part of it, and the other two parts to be equally divided among my children. And for the execution of this my last will and testament in all parcels and particulars that thereunder doth or may fall, I constitute and appoynt Mr. Joseph Hills of Mauldon, and Brother Edmund Frost, elder of the Church at Cambridge, and Mr. Henry Shrimpton of Boston, and Mr. Edward Colliers of Cambridge, who shall have full power and liberty to mannage all singular or singular things, case or cases, difficulty or difficultyes, that shall be incident or emergent during the minority of my children, viz. they or the major part of them, but in case of non-agreement among themselves, they shall bring it to my singular good friend Mr. Thomas Broughton, of Boston, who joyning with them, who by his addition shall be the greater, the case shall be quietly taken as true and righteous during the minority of my children. In virtue whereof I have hereunto [sett] my hand and seale the eighth day of ffebruary, In the year of our Lord one thousand six hundred and fifty eight."

XI.

The following facsimile of Mr. Dunster's autograph was taken from an interleaved copy of *A Concent of Scripture*, a book which belonged to him, and is now in the possession of Mr. Samuel Dunster, Attleboro'.

Natus est Jesus Chrus at Dei filius ex mar. virg: in civitate Beth-
Ann. P. Jul. 4711. Cycl. Sol. Roman. 7. Lun 18. P Constant. 5506
Cycl. Sol Graec. 18. Lun 15 Indict 1. Anno Julian 43 urb. Cond 749
Cn. Cornelio Lentulo & M. Valerio Messalino Coss. 8 Kal. Janu
arias. feria 4ta Anno Orbis Conditi 4040. post diluvium
2382. Anno ab exitu ex Aegipt 1502. Anno Judaico 3759
18 mensis Thebeth. Olymp. 194. Anno 2do Nabonassaru
746. die 6 Tybi. Anno Philippi. 322. Seleucid. Sive
Dhilcarnain 310. [illegible] 1508. Anno Actiaco
28. Choiach 28.

XII.

The following epitaph for the new monument is from the classic pen of Charles Folsom, Esq.: —

HENRICUS. DUNSTER

PRIMUS. COLLEGII. HARVARDINI. PRAESES

VIR. PIETATE. DOCTRINA. PRUDENTIA. INSIGNIS

OBIIT. SCITUATAE. AN M.DC.LIX.

HUC. TRANSLATUM. EST. CORPUS

UT. QUOD. ILLE. IN. VOTIS. HABUERAT

PROPE. ACADEMIAM. A. SE. TUM. NUTRITAM. IN. CUNABULIS

EX. RE. FAMILIARI

TUM. RITIBUS. DISCIPLINIS. LEGIBUS. INSTRUCTAM

REQUIESCERET

MONUMENTUM. HOC. INJURIA. TEMPORIS. DIRUPTAM

SOCII. AETERNUM. ACADEMIAE. DECUS. CURANTES

REFICIENDUM. JUSSERUNT. AN. M.DCCC.XLV.

INDEX.

www.ingramcontent.com/pod-product-compliance
Lightning Source LLC
LaVergne TN
LVHW020211110826
845151LV00003B/671